Managing
End User Computing
in Information Organizations

Managing
End User Computing
in Information Organizations

WILLIAM H. INMON

DOW JONES-IRWIN
Homewood, Illinois 60430

For Shirley Nowak

© DOW JONES-IRWIN, 1986

This publication is designed to provide accurate and
authoritative information in regard to the subject matter
covered. It is sold with the understanding that the
publisher is not engaged in rendering legal, accounting, or
other professional service. If legal advice or other expert
assistance is required, the services of a competent
professional person should be sought.

*From a Declaration of Principles jointly adopted by a Committee
of the American Bar Association and a Committee of Publishers.*

ISBN 0-87094-941-1

Library of Congress Catalog Card No. 86–71443

Printed in the United States of America

1 2 3 4 5 6 7 8 9 0 K 3 2 1 0 9 8 7 6

The world of end user computing is easily the fastest growing segment of data processing over the past five years and promises to grow even more over the next five. The possibilities of end user computing, the advantages and disadvantages, capabilities and limitations are all evolving today.

The potential of end user computing is great. Putting the end users' destiny into their own hands has the promise of solving many of the age-old problems in the data processing/end user relationship. But many shops are finding that creating a successful, credible, effective end user environment is difficult to accomplish, especially as the number and sophistication of the end users grow.

Many data processing managers acquire equipment, acquire software, give the end user data, then wash their hands of it. Almost universally, this abdication of responsibility has led to frustration and disappointment as the number of end users increase, and the credibility of end user computing becomes questioned.

Managing End User Computing in the Information Organizations addresses the underlying issues of success and failure for end user computing. Some of the major themes of the book are:

- End user computing is oriented toward the effective use of computing power while traditional data processing has aimed at the efficient use of the computer. The question is raised, what are the implications of the differences between computer efficiency and effectiveness?

- The technology associated with end user computing has its origins in traditional data processing. What limitations does this historical foundation impose?
- The attitudes of the end user toward end user computing vary dramatically as the budgetary responsibility shifts from data processing to the end user. What attitudes shift and what are the implications?
- End user computing is based primarily on fourth-generation language technology and spreadsheets. What are the appropriate uses of these technologies? the inappropriate uses?
- End user computing carries with it many organizational implications. How does end user computing cause the traditional organization to change? How might the organizational changes be manifested effectively?
- The achievement of credibility in the end user computing environment requires a careful architecting effort. What does the architecture entail? Why is the architecture effective? What are its major components?

 A unique feature of *Managing End User Computing in Information Organizations* is the detailed description of the architecture that is needed to support the credibility of end user computing. The components of the architecture are fully described and a detailed example follows so the reader can see firsthand how the architecture might be applied. Further chapters discuss the organizational implications of the architecture and the considerations of the end user who would build systems within the framework of the architecture.

 Another unique feature of *Managing End User Computing in the Information Organizations* is the emphasis of the cost justification and measurement of worth of end user computing.

This book is for end users, data processing personnel who must cope with the problems presented by end user computing, data administration, the chief information officer (CIO) of a company, management who must cope with the budgetary expenditures for hardware and software, and strategic planners and analysts. Each of these distinctly different organizational functions has a vital stake in the larger issues and success of end user computing.

The purpose of this book is not to describe a simple how-to-do of installing and using a piece of end user software, as many books adequately address today. Instead, this book takes a more global perspective, looking at the larger problems of effectively creating and utilizing the end user environment. Upon reading the book, the reader will be able to:

- Identify the major issues, trends, and resolution of problems of end user computing.
- Recognize the issues in his or her shop.
- Apply the generic solutions described in the book.

William H. Inmon

• •

Many thanks to Bob Jacobucci (Fireman's Fund) for his discussions on architecture and how to implement and conform to an architecture. Gail Grynuik and Melba Inmon filled in some large holes in the area of installing end user computing systems. Thanks to Kerry Yacko and Eric Bersak (Coopers and Lybrand) for their insights on spreadsheets and financial modeling. A special thanks goes to Aetna CID, with whom I exchanged ideas about my concepts of architecture and was able to share their view of architecture.

Many people from Aetna deserve thanks, but time and space permit the mention of only a few: Newell Hall, Pat Keck, John Eckert, Barry Dexter, Doug McQuilken, Karl Norris, and Bob DeRosa. And there is a final thanks to the readers of my articles on dual data base and those who attended seminars I have conducted on the subject. Their feedback has always been taken constructively and has greatly helped to shape my approach.

W. H. I.

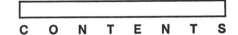

C O N T E N T S

. . . .

Section I

The End User Environment   1

What is End User Computing? The Evolution of End User Computing: *DP—An Evolving World. From a DP World to a DP/User World. Differences in Today's Environment and Yesterday's DP Environment. Different Needs. Shifts in Technology. Budgetary Differences. Backlog of Experience. Shifting Responsibility. Accelerated Evolution. Nature of the Evolution. Other Questions. Inappropriate Use of End User Computing Tools. End User Evolution—Summary.* Architecting the DSS Environment: *Processing Differences. Development Life-Cycle Differences. Gathering Requirements.* The DP to EUC Link. The EUC to DP Link: *An Emphasis on Data. Other Differences. Modes of Operation. Parameters of Success. Dual Data Bases versus "Truth" Data Bases. Some Basic Issues—Records and Sets of Records. Processing Records. Separating the Types of Processes.* Summary. Directives and Directions.

The End User Environment

Fourth-generation languages . . . are indeed the key to the promised "information society" for without those advances it will never be economically viable to use computers for anything but the most mundane and repetitive applications.

We have over 10,000 end users and have been using fourth-generation languages for over five years. If we pulled the plug on end user computing tomorrow, the only noticeable effect would be a smaller electricity bill. End user computing has had no measurable effect on the business of the corporation.

• •

The End User Environment

• •

WHAT IS END USER COMPUTING?

The technology surrounding computers was once so complex that only highly skilled technicians were able to master the complexities required to unlock the tremendous possibilities of automation. But as each year passed and the technology of computation matured, the barriers to the usage of the computer were lowered.

With the advent of fourth-generation language (4GL) technology and personal computers, the barriers to usage of the computer were lowered to the point that a whole new class of people was able to use the tools of automation. This class of people—end users—had previously been only indirectly involved in the building and shaping of computer systems. With "user friendly" 4GL technology and personal computer technology, the end user no longer had to wait on the data processing system developers to build systems.

For the purpose of this book, end user computing will include a broad range of activities—anywhere the end user directly shapes or forms his or her own computing activities will be considered to be end user computing. This broad definition of end user computing includes personal computer spread sheets, 4GL extracts and reporting, "what if" analysis, ad hoc reporting, trend analysis, demographic analysis, and the like. The activities may be run on any size processor or processors—a mainframe, a mini, or a micro. In short, end user computing includes all computing activities not developed by the classical data processing system developer.

THE EVOLUTION OF END USER COMPUTING

The end user of the 1980s is an active participant and witness to one of the most widespread and profound changes in the business landscape of the century. The changes are so profound and are happening so rapidly that the major movements and trends may not be readily discernible. Yet the importance of recognizing and understanding trends has potentially huge consequences. The possibilities for new ways to do business, more effective uses of resources, and better business decisions all appear to be tied closely to the effective usage of the tools of end user computing.

End user tools are represented by fourth-generation languages, decision support tools, spread sheets, prototypes, and the like. All of these tools invite the end user to directly participate in and/or control the processing that is going on.

But is the end user evolution (or revolution, as some claim) as simple and straightforward as merely acquiring tools, placing them in the hands of end users, and then letting the end user build systems? Only in the most simplistic, isolated case is end user computing this simple. The underlying implications—technical, organizational, and budgetary—are clearly much larger and are best understood from a high perspective.

DP—An Evolving World

In 1979 Richard Nolan wrote one of the most widely read articles in the data processing industry—"Managing the Crisis in Data Processing" (*Harvard Business Review*). In the article Nolan suggested that data processing organizations passed through different evolutionary stages. The stages—distilled from Nolan's observations of many data processing shops—have long since gained wide acceptance:

Initiation.

Contagion.

Control.

Integration.

Data administration.

Maturity.

From a DP World to a DP/User World

As the DP world turns into a DP/end user world with the advent of fourth-generation technology, there is the possibility that the end user is embarking on an evolutionary path similar to the one that DP has trod for the past three decades. By taking control of their own destinies, end users appear to be recreating an earlier data processing environment. These forces drive the end user through this widespread evolution:

Need for rapid system development.

Need to use the computer in nontraditional ways.

Costs associated with system development and subsequent system operation.

Need for consistency of data in a varied and dispersed user environment.

To some extent users are reverting to the early stages of DP maturity as described by Nolan. The end users of today appear to be entering the classical stages of initiation and contagion, but there are some major differences between today's end user environment and the infant world of DP that emerged in the 1950s and 1960s.

Differences in Today's Environment and Yesterday's DP Environment

One major difference between today's end user controlled environment and the infant data processing world of the 1950s and

1960s is in the technologies and the power of processing that are available to the end user. Under any measure the tools of technology that are available to the end user are vastly more powerful than the tools that were available to the pioneering data processing organization.

In terms of the speed with which code can be generated, there is no comparison between assembler languages and fourth-generation languages. Yet there was a day when the world was primarily assembler oriented. In terms of capabilities, there is no comparison between the 64K machine of 1965 (which was a wonder then) and today's multimegabyte machine. In terms of capacity and cost, there is no comparison between a stack of punched 80-column cards and photooptical storage. So the comparison continues.

This difference in raw power means (among other things) that the end user's stages will be greatly accelerated over that experienced by the DP organization. The early DP shops experienced many technical difficulties and setbacks with the technology that was then available, so much so that the forces that shaped the evolution of the early DP shops hid the larger forces that were at work.

Different Needs

A second major difference between the emerging end user environment and the pioneering DP environment is in the *type* of need facing the end user. The primary need faced by the end user is for decision support-type systems. These systems are generally small (relative to their DP brethren), quick to construct, and easy to change. There is a fundamental difference between the end user systems of today and the DP systems of yesterday in terms of size, usage, and criticality.

End user systems are designed to *manage* the company, and yesterday's DP systems were designed to *run* the company. The difference is the classical one between decision support systems and operational systems. (Note: Later there will be a discussion of what happens when the user wishes to write operational systems with fourth-generation end user tools.) This major difference in the functions performed by the end user and the functions performed by DP yesterday is relevant to the user passing through the stages of evolution.

The relevancy of the difference between end user systems and operational systems is complicated by the fact that the forces of the end user evolution are decelerated or accelerated in different ways. For example, since the decision support systems built by the user are not sensitive to the day-to-day operations of the company, there is less pressure to build the system quickly than if the systems were crucial to the everyday running of the company. Suppose the end user is comparing this year's account activity with last year's. As important as the comparison is, the company will not cease to operate if the decision support system is not created this week. But in an operational environment, the pressures for quick development are commonplace because part or all of the company will be unable to function if the system isn't built. The result is that there is less pressure for fast systems development by the end user because of the nature of the systems being built. The lack of operational criticality of end user systems then eases one of the traditional forces of evolution—the need to build systems quickly.

From a different perspective, across *all* departments that are building decision support systems, the pressure to evolve into higher evolutionary stages of end user computing will be even greater. For example, when upper management asks three or four related departments for information on which to make a decision, and three or four very disjointed answers are returned, there will be a great and immediate demand by upper management to resolve the differences between departments. This pressure for integrated end user systems will come very early (relative to its appearance in the DP evolution) and will cause end users to evolve quickly.

Shifts in Technology

Another major difference between the emerging end users environment and the pioneering DP environment is in the orientation toward technology—How technical is the environment? The DP world of yesterday was (and still is to some extent) very "technician" oriented. At the heart of the DP department are operating system technicians, network technicians, data base technicians, operations technicians, and the like. Without these technicians the world of DP would probably not turn. However, in today's user environment, there is a very strong motivation to depart from a technical orientation.

The end user's world has been shaped by "user friendliness," which reduces the technical orientation of the environment. Even in the cases where "user friendliness" is more fancy than fact, there is no doubt that the end user environment is much simpler, much cleaner, and much easier to manage than the pioneering, technically oriented DP environment. The move from a technological orientation toward user friendliness means fewer obstacles between end user and the systems the end user wishes to create. There is no doubt that the removal of technical barriers will greatly accelerate the user's progression through the evolutionary phases.

Budgetary Differences

Another *major* difference (in fact, probably the most profound difference) between the emerging end user's environment and the DP environment of yesterday is in budgetary control. In yesterday's DP environment it was the DP department that bought equipment and software, and the department operated as a service organization. In most shops the end user considered DP services and equipment to be a free resource (sometimes accounted for in what is termed "funny money"). To this day, many end users still have not made the connection between the bottom line of profitability of their company and the resources consumed by hardware and software when DP is in charge of the budget.

But as control of systems—the building, running, and maintenance of systems—is passed to the end user, the responsibility for the budget is passed along as well. Most micro processors and end user computing software is being sold to the end user, not DP. Now the budgetary choice of dollar is coming directly out of the end user's pocket. With direct budgetary responsibility, the end user makes a connection between the choice of purchasing a PC versus upgrading the carpet in the end user's office. This budgetary shift of control—from DP to end user— greatly helps to accelerate end user evolution.

In the shops where DP still pays for the resources consumed in the end user-controlled environment, the result is deceleration of the end user through the stages of evolution. In fact, the strategy of DP funding of an end user-controlled environment has many negative connotations (for all parties concerned).

Backlog of Experience

Another important difference between the emerging end user environment and the pioneering DP environment is in the backlog of available experience. In yesterday's DP world, there was simply no previous experience on which managers, technicians, or anyone else could rely. Everything was brand new. Patterns were hard to recognize, trends were not apparent, and sound practices often could not be distinguished from unsound ones. The criteria for success was not distinguishable, and the result was a very strange set of priorities and practices in many cases. In today's world (for user and DP alike), there is a basis for comparison. One hopes the experiences of the past three decades have not been lost. The availability of a backlog of experience should steer the end user away from grossly incorrect decisions and reduce learning by trial and error. Today's "user friendly" tools and the lessening dependence on technicians will greatly help the user through the initial learning stages. However, it is doubtful that the sophistication of end user tools will help the user through the latter learning stages. The latter stages of the data processing organization's evolution are primarily related to organizational discipline, not technology.

The issue of control is complicated by the fact that data processing is usually centralized (to one degree or another), and the different user departments are typically not centralized. Control (which is difficult in any case) becomes very difficult in the face of decentralization. To make matters worse, end user decentralization is often along political lines, and political boundaries have traditionally been the most difficult over which to exert organizational discipline.

Shifting Responsibility

Another difference between the end user's world and the pioneering world of data processing is that the end user can no longer hold the data processing system developers responsible for not producing systems. By taking control of hardware and software, the end user by default takes the responsibility for producing results. The only responsibility left to DP is to provide data. Furthermore, the consistency of processing across the community of end user becomes the responsibility of the end user, not DP. When upper management begins to address the classical problems of control and integration of processing among several end user departments, the end users will no longer be able to point to DP as the culprit.

Important to the speed with which the user goes through the different stages of evolution is just how far the DP department has evolved. If the DP department is still in the early stages of control, then it is unlikely that the end user can evolve much further than DP. (In this case DP *may well be* holding up the end user's evolution.) The nature of the end user system is decision support, and those systems normally are fed by operational data. If the operational data is uncontrolled and unintegrated, then the end user may have a very shaky foundation on which to build. In this case the end user may well be a significant factor in furthering or hastening the evolution of DP. Most DP shops should have evolved beyond the early stages of Nolan's evolution.

Accelerated Evolution

If it is true then that the end user is entering the stages of an evolution, then it is clear that the factors at work in today's world will greatly accelerate the end user through those stages (at least the early stages). The factors relevant to the user's accelerated evolution are:

More powerful equipment, technologies.

A different set of needs (DSS versus operational).

Less technical orientation.

A shift in budgetary control.

The existence of a backlog of experience.

Nature of the Evolution

An interesting question is whether or not the stages of evolution appropriate to DP are also the same stages that are appropriate to the end user. If the end user were literally creating a new DP department, then Nolan's stages would probably apply. Yet the very nature of what the end user is doing is fundamentally different from what DP does. So it is entirely possible that the end user will go through a somewhat modified set of stages of the evolution. The stages of initiation and contagion are being experienced today by the user, and the user is making rapid progress through those stages. It is in the control stage that the user will most likely have a variant of the experiences of DP; and as the user approaches the stages of integration and data administration, it is highly likely that those stages will vary significantly from those experienced by DP.

Other Questions

Whether or not the end user's evolution through different stages of evolution is going to be accelerated is an interesting point. The mere fact that the end user will be going through different stages brings up some interesting and related questions. Some of these questions are:

- What about the continuing evolution in today's DP shop?
- What about companies that do not shift budgetary control from DP to end user for end user computing?
- What about companies that allow end users to build operational systems with decision support tools?

Today's DP shop will neither cease to exist nor cease to evolve. The advent of end user computing is complementary to the processing that DP does. In fact the needs for DP services will continue to increase, but DP will be doing primarily operational activities. The line between operational and DSS systems will become clearly delineated over time—DP manages the operational aspects of the business, and the end user manages the decision support activities, and within DP's domain the forces of evolution as described by Nolan will continue to operate. The departure of decision support systems from DP's domain will cause but a momentary relaxation of the evolutionary forces at work in the DP environment.

A second issue concerns the shift of budget control from the DP department to the end user department. It is natural for the end user to assume responsibility of the budget as the end user takes control. However, if data processing is still saddled with buying the software and hardware for the end user, while the end user otherwise controls the environment, data processing is placed in an untenable position from the standpoint of fiscal responsibility. For the end user to experience the forces of evolution and consequently to mature, there must be a realization that services and equipment have a price tag attached. As long as DP is paying that price, the end user will not readily make the connection. So it is essential that as the control of the environment passes to the end user, the budgetary responsibility is likewise passed.

One type of company (which is becoming increasingly rare) will probably not evolve under any set of circumstances—the company with the "infinite budget" approach to DP. In DP's infancy (Nolan's initiation stage), many companies required what seemed to be a never-ending increase in budget. As long as DP was establishing itself within the company, top management had an open-handed attitude toward the budget. In most shops a major part of the DP maturation process was in cost justification. In many smaller, marginally profitable companies, this maturation occurred quickly, of necessity. In larger companies (especially regulated or highly profitable ones), an open-handed attitude remained long after the point at which other companies had discarded the attitude. A few regulated companies even sought to *increase* DP spending beyond normal growth rates in order to raise the regulated rates at which the company operated. In these cases data processing has always operated as if there were no end to the budget available. Organizations having no apparent budgetary constraint have little incentive to mature, and there is no reason to believe their end users will mature any more quickly than have their DP departments.

Inappropriate Use of End User Computing Tools

Later chapters will discuss the trade-off between development and operational costs in traditional and end user computing environments. Based upon the economics, there are powerful incentives to build systems quickly with end user computing tools, but not *all* systems are economical to build and operate using end user computing software. The flexibility of end user computing software comes at a price. There is an overhead associated with flexibility. For systems that are executed very frequently—such as operational systems—the overhead may be more than the end user is willing to pay.

An interesting issue arises when the end user attempts to use fourth-generation tools to build operational systems. The result in many cases has been unparalleled spiraling of hardware costs. When the end user attempts to build operational systems with tools that entail much overhead, the associated hardware costs can very quickly cause the user to change the focus of the type of system built. At the outset the end user wishes to build systems quickly, but once the system is built, the priorities of the end user change and the end user wishes the system to run quickly and efficiently. Unfortunately for large-scaled operational systems, the trade-off is usually mutually exclusive between end user computing software (i.e., systems that can be built quickly) and operationally oriented software (i.e., systems that run quickly and efficiently). A final issue concerns the nature of the end user's evolution itself. Is the end user evolution necessary? Can the end user leap frog from one stage to another? Does the move to end user computing merely signal a change in control within the organization, or is it symptomatic of a more profound change? Does the end user movement herald a clear delineation in the roles of DP and the user? Will all end users experience the evolution? What lies beyond maturity? How will the DP and end user evolutions affect each other?

End User Evolution—Summary

In summary, by taking control of his or her own data processing destiny, the end user appears to be entering into the beginning of a series of different stages of evolution similar to the stages of evolution outlined by Nolan through which DP passes. It is anticipated that the user will pass through these stages in an accelerated fashion for a variety of reasons. Yet simply because the end user has departed from the DP department does not mean the DP department will cease to exist or cease to evolve. Finally, the departure of the end user will cause the role of DP to be that of caretaker of the operational systems, and the role of the end user will be that of caretaker of the decision support systems.

ARCHITECTING THE DSS ENVIRONMENT

Certainly the origins of end user computing are steeped in the traditional data processing department—at least insofar as technology and practices are concerned. The conjecture that the end user is reinventing in whole or in part the traditional DP department and will experience its own evolution is interesting. However, there are some very major differences between the traditional DP environment and the end user environment that greatly affect the effectiveness of end user computing. Some of the major differences will be explored.

Processing Differences

The essence of end user computing is autonomy of processing. As such, for most analytical tasks, there is "an answer"—a final

---

F   I   G   U   R   E   1-1

Iterative Loop for End User Computing

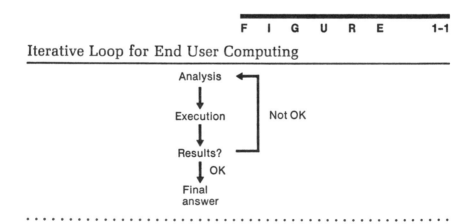

resolution to the question being posed. Typically the "answer" is arrived at after multiple iterations of analysis. Each analysis refines the previous effort until the desired result is achieved. Figure 1–1 depicts a typical reiterated loop for DSS end user processing.

Contrast the type of processing done in Figure 1–1 with the type of processing typically done by the data processing department, which involves the accessing, storing, or updating of data. Data is typically stored on magnetic tape or disk (direct access storage device, or DASD). Data is entered by means of a cathode ray tube, card reader, or other device used for input and output of data. The processing of the data is done by the computer. Figure 1–2 shows a simple data processing system.

Contrast the processing done in Figures 1–1 and 1–2. In the case of end user systems, there is a desired result to be obtained—an "answer"—that is the objective of the end user. In the case of data processing systems, the purpose of the system is to serve as a vehicle in the furthering of some business process, and there is no "answer" per se that is achieved. The most fundamental difference between end user computing and traditional processing is that the end user builds systems to arrive at some conclusion, whereas the data processor builds systems to enhance the day-to-day running of the business of the enter-

F   I   G   U   R   E   1-2

A Simple DP System

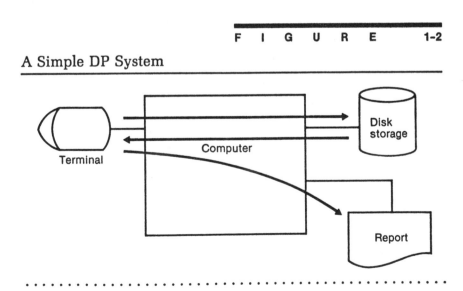

prise. This difference can be stated another way. The difference is one between the effective use of the computer and the efficient use of the computer. The end user desires to achieve more effective ways to conduct his or her business, and the data processor wishes to achieve more efficient ways to accomplish the business of the organization. The difference between effectiveness and efficiency permeates itself in many places.

It is possible to use end user computing tools for other than effectiveness. In some cases end user computing tools have been used to produce classical data processing systems. When the intent is to build a prototype of classical data processing systems, end user tools can be very beneficial. When the intent is actually to build replacements for classical data processing systems (sometimes called production or operational systems) in the face of a large volume of data, a large amount of processing, and short response time, the result is usually frustration, for a variety of reasons (as will be discussed later). In other cases where volume of data, volume of processing, and criticality of response time are not issues, end user computing tools can satisfactorily replace traditional systems.

Development Life-Cycle Differences

The development life cycle of end user computing then is quite different than that of data processing systems, due in no small part to the major differences in the types of processing done. Figure 1–3 shows the two life cycles in terms of the functions done throughout the life cycle. Figure 1–3 makes clear the fact that the data processing life cycle is much more complex (in terms of technology and activities done) than is the end user computing life cycle. In the data processing system life cycle are found such activities as system integration, programming, and physical design. Given the complexity of the tools that are found in the data processing environment, it is no surprise that the development process is tedious.

Now consider the end user computing environment. The tools of end user computing are geared for flexibility and rapid system development. Thus iterating an end user computing design is an entirely rational approach. Of course, in the traditional data processing system environment, no designer would

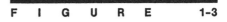

F I G U R E   1-3

DP and End User Development Life Cycles, by Function

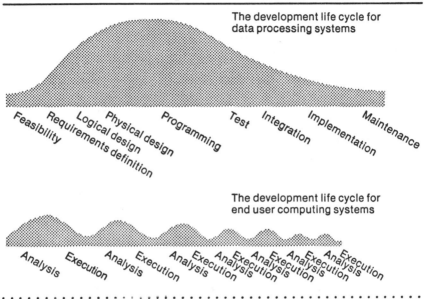

The development life cycle for
data processing systems

Feasibility Requirements definition Logical design Physical design Programming Test Integration Implementation Maintenance

The development life cycle for
end user computing systems

Analysis Execution Analysis Execution Analysis Execution Analysis Execution Analysis Execution Analysis Execution Analysis Execution

think of iterating a systems design. It is not necessary to carefully specify requirements at the outset of an end user computing project as it is for data processing projects because any requirement not taken into consideration by the end user can be factored into the requirements of the next iteration of the design.

Also note that the end user computing function of "execute" (as shown in Figure 1–3) encompasses *many* functions found separately in the data processing system development life cycle. "Execute" includes such activities as physical design, programming, test, and so on. Although the comparison of the two system development life cycles is interesting from the standpoint of functionality, there are even more marked differences when the total resource utilization (personnel, hardware, etc.) is considered, as shown by Figure 1–4.

Figure 1–4 shows that the typical data processing project requires *much* more personnel and hardware and is done over a much longer period than the end user computing project. Because of the inflexibility of the tools used in the data processing

Comparison of DP and End User Life Cycles, Drawn to Scale

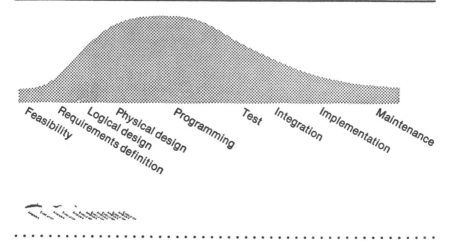

environment, the requirements for data processing systems must be rigidly and completely defined. By the same token, because of the flexibility of the tools of end user computing, there is not a great need to capture all requirements in the first few iterations of end user computation. Figure 1–5 illustrates the difference in the need for requirement definitions.

Gathering Requirements

The importance of the flexibility afforded by end user computing tools shows up nowhere better than in Figure 1–5. The amount of work required to gather up all system requirements as done in the data processing environment is *huge*. Furthermore, given the number of requirements, their mere organization and prioritization is a large task. It is quite normal for some requirements to have changed before all are noted. However, in the end user computing environment, requirements can be gathered heuristically. Beginning with a basic analysis, the end user is able to selectively add (or delete) requirements from one iteration of the analysis to the next.

Another interesting perspective in the traditional DP environment is that requirements are gathered by DP professionals.

F   I   G   U   R   E   1-5

Illustrative Comparison of Need for Requirements Definitions

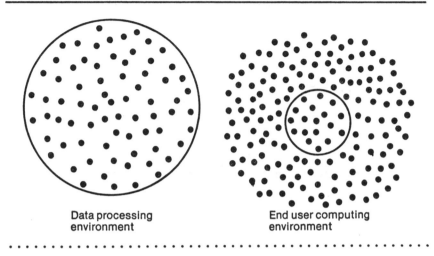

Data processing environment

End user computing environment

In essence, experienced systems people learn the business of the organization. Such a learning curve is long and tedious. With end user computing, the reverse is true; the users, who already know their business, must learn systems. Given the user friendliness of end user software, this learning curve is significantly less than the learning curve experienced by the DP systems staff. In other words, it is much more efficient to teach systems to end users than it is to teach business to systems people.

The economics gained by flexible tools and the ability to heuristically develop requirements are obvious, but it should be mentioned that the flexibility of end user computing comes at a price. The cost is best illustrated in terms of the utilization of a processor while operating on a typical data processing job stream and while operating on a typical end user computing job stream. Figure 1-6 shows the resource utilization that occurs for end user computing and for data processing.

In general, data processing machine utilization tends to be fairly static; that is, fairly constant. There are small variations in moment-to-moment machine utilization, but overall machine use remains constant. On the other hand, end user computing

F   I   G   U   R   E   1-6

Resource Utilization: DP and End User Comparison

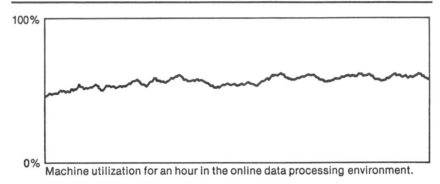

Machine utilization for an hour in the online data processing environment.

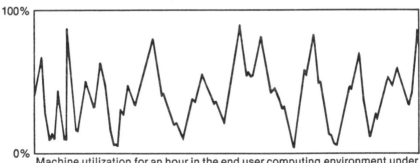

Machine utilization for an hour in the end user computing environment under a moderate machine load.

tends to heavily use the machine one moment and to lightly use the machine the next moment. Furthermore, the length of time the end user machine is heavily used is indeterminate. The blatantly different machine uses stem from the fact that data processing activities tend to be very structured, and end user computing activities tend to be very unstructured. The structured data processing activity profile occurs because the user of the system can do only what the programs designed and written by the programmer allow him or her to do. Furthermore, these structured programs are carefully designed so that they do a limited amount of work for each user interaction. The result is that machine resources are used in a predictable fashion.

The end user environment allows the end user to write programs and to have full autonomy to do processing as desired, unconstrained by any structure superimposed by data processing. The result of unstructured processing is a very different pattern of machine utilization.

Another way of looking at this difference between end user computing and data processing is that the capacity projections of data processing are a function of the number of activities being executed, and the capacity projections of the end user depend on *both* the number of activities being executed *and* the nature of the activities executed. The net result is that the capacity needs of end user computing are much more difficult to project than the capacity needs of data processing. Because end user capacity needs are so difficult to project, there is a natural gravitation of the end user to the micro processor environment, wherein the end user does not have to worry about what other end users are doing in order to do end user computations.

The significant differences between end user computing and traditional DP computing can be summarized by:

Intent of the processing.

Structure of the processing.

Development life cycle.

Need to capture requirements.

Despite the major differences in the types of processing, data processing and end user computing should work in a harmonious, complementary fashion. The relationship of data processing and end user computing is shown by the feedback loop depicted in Figure 1–7. The figure shows that data processing feeds end user computing and vice versa. Data processing is the function by which the day-to-day informational activities of the organization are run. Indeed in banks and insurance companies it is often said that the computer *is* the line organization. End user computing then is used to manage the organization.

THE DP TO EUC LINK

The lower part of the feedback loop as shown in Figure 1–7 is the link from DP to end user computing. This relationship is typified by the flow of much data, usually at a detailed level. Data processing keeps track of the many events that occur in

F I G U R E 1-7

The Data Processing–End User Computing–Business
Interaction Loop

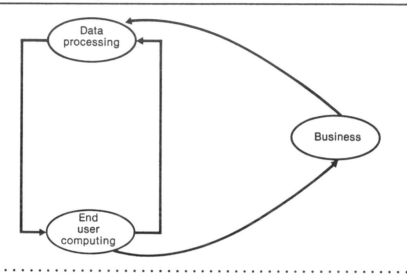

the organization. The detail is necessarily at a low level because
this is the level at which day-to-day detailed decisions are made
as to how to run the company. Can the company cash a check?
When did the auto policy expire? What assembly was produced
by line XYZ on October 13? These pieces of information are
stored and used within the data processing environment. On a
periodic basis, data processing collects relevant details and
ships them to the end user. The end user may also receive detailed information from external sources, such as commercial
data banks. In general there is a healthy amount of data flowing
over this link, and the flow of data is done on a periodic basis;
that is, it is regularly scheduled.

THE EUC TO DP LINK

Not so neatly defined as the data processing to end user computing link is the end user computing to data processing link (although this link is every bit as important). Some of the forms
this link may take are:

Correction of information. An error is discovered in the examination of detailed data flowing from the data processing environment. The detailed correction is made in the data processing environment.

Environmental changes. Complete or satisfactory analysis in the end user computing environment is not able to be done because of incomplete or inaccurate information flowing from the DP environment. As a consequence more complete information needs are recognized, and data is gathered in the data processing environment, thus making the data processing environment more effective.

The most effective form the end user computing to data processing link takes is that of causing better business decisions to be made, which in turn expands the business, which places a heavier load on existing data processing systems. The link from end user computing to DP takes two forms—a direct link and an indirect link. The direct link occurs when an end user produces a system that either has wide usefulness and applicability beyond the end user and/or when the system can be run more economically in the DP environment. In this case, the system leaves the domain of end user computing and enters the domain of traditional DP. Prototypes, trend analysis and the like are forms of direct feedback from end user computing to DP. The indirect link between end user computing and DP occurs as the end user causes management to make better decisions, which in turn affect the business of the organization. As the business prospers, the load on the DP systems heightens and is measured once again by end user computing systems. The indirect feedback from end user systems to DP systems is typified by financial models and projections, "what if" analysis, demographic analysis, and so forth.

An Emphasis on Data

One consequence of the fact that system requirements for end user processing do not have to be as rigidly determined as for data processing systems is that there is more of an emphasis on data and less on processing for end user computing.

In the typical data processing system, the analyst must determine down to a low level of detail what the processing and data requirements for the system are. It is fair to say that in the data processing environment there is equal emphasis—50–50— on data and processes. But in the end user computing environment, there is an emphasis on data, for several reasons:

Processes can be changed easily if algorithmic changes must be made.

Because processes can be changed so easily, end user computing often comprises many iterations of processing to achieve the final result.

Even though processing can be changed easily, if data on which the processes operate is either unavailable or incorrect, then no amount of processing flexibility will suffice.

Figure 1–8 illustrates the difference in emphasis between the data processing environment and the end user computing environment. However, the differences between the two environments do not end with a shift of emphasis on data and processes. There are other fundamental differences in the two

F   I   G   U   R   E   1–8

DP and EUC: Comparing Emphasis on Data and Processes

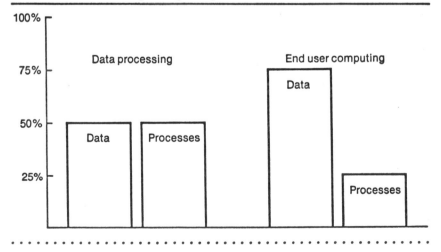

environments, especially data usage. Some of the major differences are:

Level of detail. In the data processing environment, there is a real need for detail. Consider a typical data processing system, such as bank teller processing. When Cathy Klein wants to withdraw $50 from her checking account, the teller needs to know specific account information (about Cathy Klein), specific balance information (about Cathy's balance), and so forth. In the end user computing environment, there is normally no need for specific detailed information. For example, suppose the end user analyst for marketing wants to compare this month's teller activities to last month's. For this kind of summary analysis, it does not particularly matter what Cathy Klein's balance is at any moment in time, or for that matter whether or not Cathy withdraws $50. All of the detail concerning Cathy will be summarized with other accounts such that the details of any one account are not terribly important.

Timeliness of information. Using the previous example of a bank withdrawal and a monthly account analysis, the timeliness of information is easily illuminated. When Cathy Klein goes to the teller window, it is both to her advantage and to the bank's to have her detailed data current to the second. If the bank has received a deposit from her employer at 12:00 P.M., it will displease Cathy if the bank cannot or will not cash her check at 1:00 P.M. Furthermore, if the bank does cash Cathy's check at 1:00 P.M., and if Cathy mistakenly tries to use her ATM (Automated Teller Machine) at 2:00 P.M. for a larger amount than is appropriate, then the bank is at risk. Thus it is that for data processing systems the timeliness of data at a detailed level is of paramount importance. Now consider the issue of timeliness and end user computing. For the purpose of monthly comparisons of account activity, the issue of timeliness is almost nonexistent. As long as each month can be summed up and is accurate up to the moment of the monthly close of books, timeliness of data—certainly data at a detailed level—is a nonissue. The data is captured by means of a "snapshot" that is taken for the month. The snapshot reflects the data as of one moment in time. Once the snapshot is taken, the data will not change.

Timeliness of data, then, in the end user environment where snapshots of data are taken has a completely different meaning and perspective than timeliness of data in the data processing environment.

Wide access to data. In the data processing environment, it is important that data be available to a wide number of users. If Cathy Klein wishes to enter any branch of the bank and go to the window of any teller in the bank, she is free to do so, and Cathy should expect that *any* teller will be able to service her requests. However, in the end user computing environment, there is increasingly limited access to data. Once the monthly activity for the bank is stripped, the account analyst strips off a subset of that data. For further analysis the data become more summarized and refined. In the final analysis, the bank officers and the analyst see the results of the end user processing. The final results are available to and are of interest to only a very few people.

Types of processing done. In the data processing environment there is a high degree of structure to the processing that is done, and in the end user environment there is very little structure. In the data processing environment, when Cathy Klein walks up to the teller window to cash a check, the teller can verify Cathy's balance. The teller may be able to do a few other things for Cathy, such as tell her the sums of the last three checks that have been cashed, the last deposit, and so forth. Yet after all is said and done, the bank teller has a limited amount of information that can be offered to Cathy. Furthermore, the teller is restricted to the usage of the system to the ways specified by the system developer and programmer. In other words, the teller uses preprogrammed routines, created by a programmer. The teller's work on the computer is prestructured by the systems developer. Now consider the analyst doing the monthly account analysis. A certain portion of the analyst's work is fairly routine, such as stripping snapshot data from the data processing data. But once the routine work is done, the analyst may do much work not structured along any given lines. The analyst may ask such questions as these:

"For all accounts from branches A, B, and C, what deposits were more than $1,000?"

"For all electronic funds transfer, has this month's volume differed from last month's by more than 10 percent?"

"For all dormant accounts for last month, were the accounts also dormant this month?"

The analyst has the full freedom to do whatever processing is desired and is not subject to a predetermined pattern of usage of the computer.

Amount of data. The total amount of data found in end user computing and data processing varies considerably. When Cathy Klein asks a teller to access her data, only a small amount of data is used; but Cathy's account represents only one of many accounts serviced by operational systems. Taken collectively there is much account data in the data processing environment. However, in end user computing, there is relatively very little data because data is summarized and selectively stripped. In analyzing monthly data about account activity, the analyst is working with a relatively small amount of data. (Some types of end user computing, such as actuarial analysis, do not necessarily fit with this criterion.)

From a perspective of data, the following represents a list of the major fundamental differences between data processing and end user computing:

Level of detail.

Timeliness of information.

Public access to data.

Structured/unstructured processing of data.

Amounts of data.

Data use is only one major difference between data processing and end user computing. There are major differences in the processes that operate on the data as well. The principal difference in processing stems in the reusability of a process. The processes that operate in data processing are almost exclusively processes that are to be used many times. Whether the process is a program that produces a report or an online transaction that updates a data base, the intent is for multiple usages of the program. For end user computing, it is quite normal for a program to be written, used once, then never used again. In other cases a program is written and then is constantly modified so that many different variations of the same program are executed. One form of end user computing does occur repetitively when a program periodically strips and/or refines, merges, and restructures data from the data processing environment.

Other Differences

A major difference between the DP and the end user computing environments is control. In the data processing environment, the end user is part of a community that uses a common facility. There are generally many users served by the data processing department. End users must "wait their turns in line." Furthermore, since the budget is in the domain of data processing, there is little the end user can do to get results. In short, given the size and centralized nature of data processing, the end user has relatively little direct control of the proceedings. With end user computing, the end user is armed with his or her own computer, tools designed for simple usage, and data. The end user is in control, and this shift is much more than psychological.

Modes of Operation

The differences then between end user computing and data processing are many and are at the heart of the environment— the data and processes that form the very fiber of the environment. In fact, the differences between data processing and end user computing are so deep that these two environments can be considered to be separate *modes of operation*. A mode of operation is a collection of processes that collectively operate in a similar fashion but operate distinctly differently from other modes of operation.

Certain major implications stem from the fact that end user computing and data processing are distinctly separate modes of operation:

There are different ongoing organizational units controlling each mode.

There are different physical configurations appropriate to each mode.

There are different software packages that apply to each mode.

There are different expectations and parameters of success for each mode.

Parameters of Success

The last point strikes at the profound differences between data processing and end user computing. Contrast the different parameters of success for the two modes of operations.

Data processing	*End user computing*
Ability to quickly build systems.	Ability to build systems with minimal technical background.
Ability to accurately build systems.	Ability to change systems quickly.
Quick response time (for online systems).	Ability to get at data, select data, and refine data.
High percentage of availability (for online systems).	Operational efficiency.
Operational efficiency.	
Integrity of data and processing.	

From the above list, it is seen that the parameters of success are entirely different from one environment to the next. Only operational efficiency is on both lists, but even operational efficiency has entirely different connotations in each environment. In data processing, operational efficiency refers to the cost-effective handling of many transactions, many reports, and the management of much data. In end user computing, operational efficiency is simply measured by comparing the cost of processing versus the worth of the answer that has been derived.

Dual Data Bases versus "Truth" Data Bases

Much controversy has resulted in the philosophy of whether the modes of operation should be separate or combined. There is a certain intellectual appeal to the notion that a single data base—a "truth" data base—should serve both data processing and end user computing needs. If it were possible to have a single data base serve both modes of operation:

Data, at the detailed level, would always be accurate up to the second.

No processing would be required to pass data from one mode of operation to the next.

In fact, in light of very small amounts of data and very small amounts of processing, it is possible to enjoy a single data base that serves both modes of operation at the same time. But as the amount of data grows and/or as the amount of processing to be done against the data grows, the differences between the modes of operation are such that a single processor is unable to do both data processing and end user computing *at the same time.*

One solution is to "time slice" or "duplex" the processing. A common form of "duplexing" occurs where data processing is done during the daytime and end user computing is done at night on the same machine. The same data base, the same machine, and (one hopes) the same software can be used. Depending on the time of day, either data processing or end user computing is being done, but not both at the same time. This scenario is uncomfortable for the end user in that the end user is relegated to using the data during nonnormal working hours.

A third possibility is to physically remove the data from one processor and push the data to another processor. This entails an extract (or "snapshot") process. Such an arrangement allows data processing to occur during the day *and* end user computing to occur *at the same time* without any interference. The price of this arrangement is the redundancy of data and the loss of timeliness as data is extracted from data processing. But given the nature of end user computing, the duplication of data and the loss of timeliness present small obstacles. When the two modes of operation are physically separated, it is assumed that there remains a single *system of record.* The system of record implies that there is a single source of data at the detailed level. Data is updated in one place only—at the source. Wherever else the data is used, it is copied from the source. In 99 percent of the cases, the system of record will reside in the data processing mode of operation. Figure 1–9 illustrates the three hardware configurations that are commonly found. Figure 1–10 shows that the system of record becomes an issue only when the "dual data base" approach is used. However, more issues surround the different modes of operation than the issue of data. The issue of usage of data is another major dividing line between the operational and the end user computing modes of operation.

Some Basic Issues—Records and Sets of Records

A record is a single unit of like information stored in a computer or on a medium that is accessible to a computer, such as disk storage or magnetic tape. A typical record for an employee might include employee number, employee name, department the employee works for, date of employment, and job classification. A typical record for a manufacturing company might include part number, time and date the part was received, the quantity received, and the manufacturing line. Depending on the software being used, the record may be called a "tuple," a "file," a "segment," and so forth.

Generally, records are related to other records. For example, an employment record may be related to a departmental work history record, a personnel record, or a key employee recognition record. A manufacturing record for a part may be related to an inventory record, a shipping record, or a quality control record. In other cases a record can be considered to be related to other like records. For example, all employee records make up the collective work force of a company. Or all the manufacturing records of a company collectively make up a view of the productivity and output of the company.

Processing Records

In most cases end user computing software processes data in terms of sets of records, or set-at-a-time. Traditional nonend user computing processes data record-at-a-time, such as CO-BOL and Fortran. Some profound implications to end user

Three Common Hardware Configurations for Mode of Operation

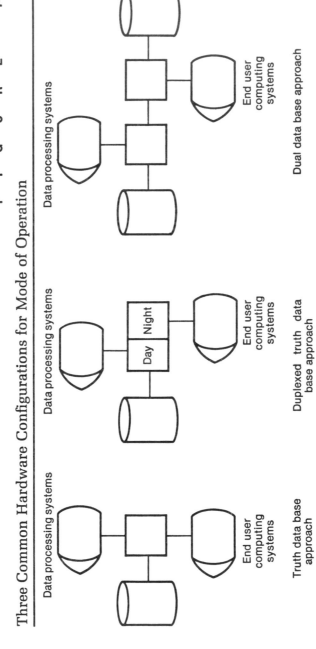

F I G U R E   1-9

Relating a System of Record to the Dual Data Base Approach

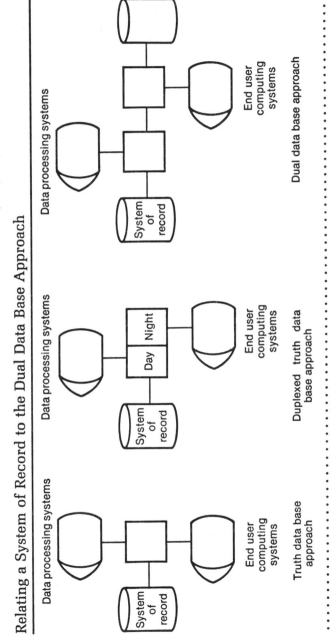

Data processing systems

Data processing systems

Data processing systems

System of record

System of record

System of record

Day | Night

End user computing systems

End user computing systems

End user computing systems

Truth data base approach

Duplexed truth data base approach

Dual data base approach

F I G U R E   1-10

computing are not obvious because of this seemingly innocent difference between processing philosophies. From the standpoint of "user friendliness," end user computing is much easier and is much more flexible in adapting the philosophy of set-at-a-time record processing. It is natural for the end user to think (for many kinds of processing) in terms of sets of data, not individual records.

Set-at-a-Time and Record-at-a-Time Processing at the Syntax and Execution Level

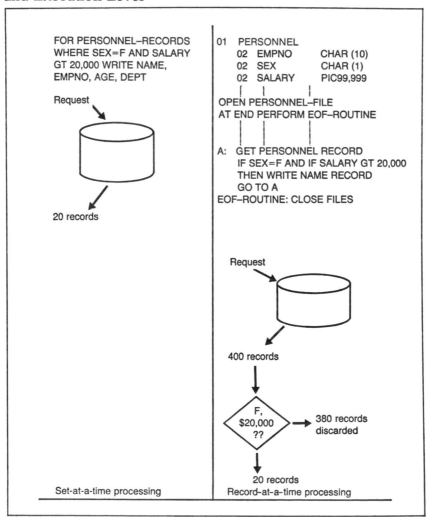

It is unquestionably user friendly to free the end user from having to manipulate data one record-at-a-time. The end user does not have to worry about finding the first record or what to do after the last record has been located. The end user does not have to worry about locating data that is poorly organized, and so forth. Furthermore, given that most end user computing software is easily able to join related records (such as employee-personnel records, or manufacturing-inventory records), the end user does not have to worry about the logic or work required to "join" related records.

The software for end user computing, for these reasons, then is very useful for the quick construction of systems and for the quick changes that are made. In other words, if productivity is equivalent to the speed of coding that can be achieved, then end user computing software represents a much more productive tool than traditional software. Because end user computing software operates on data a set-at-a-time, it is indeterminate how many records are processed. Given a simple end user computing statement:

FOR INVENTORY–FILE
WHERE PART NO. CREATE.DATE = '091085'
ADD + 1 TO CTR

it is unclear how many inventory file records are to be accessed. Will this statement access one record? Ten records? One thousand records? It is impossible to look at the statement and say how many total records are to be accessed without first knowing information about the amount of data and the organization of data being operated on. (In standard DP parlance, the simple query that has been depicted is a "data driven process.") Thus performance of processing becomes an issue because end user computing typically causes an unpredictable amount of resources to be used. If the computer must access one or two records, most likely performance will not be harmed. But if the computer must access 1,000, 10,000, or more records for a single end user request, then it is a good bet that performance will be harmed.

There is a further complication with performance. It is one thing for a computer to perform poorly because of a single request. If all that is hurt is performing a single request then performance really isn't a problem. The performance issue

becomes a real problem in the face of many activities attempting to use the computer at once. Consider a simple, but appropriate, analogy as depicted by Figure 1–11. There are two
queues for a bank depicted in the figure. In each queue are customers who desire to transact business with the bank. You arrive at the back of the queue (and are denoted by a square
around your x.) In queue 1 you have in front of you only people
who wish to cash a check. Cashing a check requires only a few
moments of the teller's time. Consequently, your passage
through queue 1 is fast and pleasant. Now consider what happens in queue 2. In front of you are people who only want to
cash checks and one person who wishes to reconcile six
months' worth of account activity. Needless to say the teller is
tied up for a long time, and you wait and wait and wait. The
analogy described here is equivalent (on a simplistic basis) with
what happens when set-at-a-time processing is mixed with

F I G U R E   1–11

Bank Queue Analogy

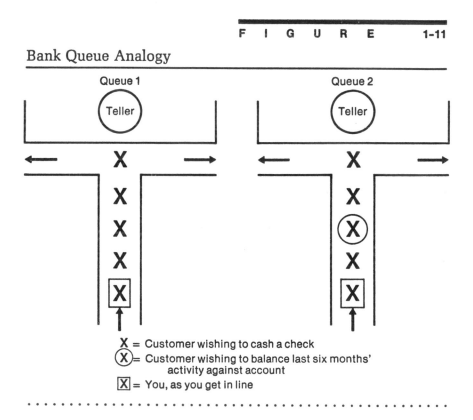

X = Customer wishing to cash a check
(X) = Customer wishing to balance last six months'
           activity against account
[X] = You, as you get in line

record-at-a-time processing. Record-at-a-time processing corresponds to cashing a check, and set-at-a-time processing corresponds to reconciling six months of activity. The negative impact of performance is felt not just for the set-at-a-time processing that monopolizes the processor, but by all the record-at-

---

End user computing uses the computer to produce an "answer," and production processing uses the computer as a vehicle for the more efficient transaction of business.

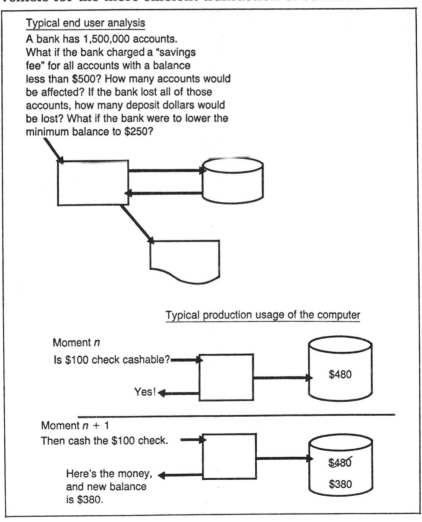

Typical end user analysis

A bank has 1,500,000 accounts.
What if the bank charged a "savings fee" for all accounts with a balance less than $500? How many accounts would be affected? If the bank lost all of those accounts, how many deposit dollars would be lost? What if the bank were to lower the minimum balance to $250?

Typical production usage of the computer

Moment *n*
Is $100 check cashable?

$480

Yes!

Moment *n* + 1
Then cash the $100 check.

$480
$380

Here's the money, and new balance is $380.

a-time processes that are queued behind the set-at-a-time process.

Separating the Types of Processes

It is a temptation to say that set-at-a-time processing that uses many resources should be identified as it enters the queue so that it can be placed in a special queue reserved for nothing but resource intensive set-at-a-time processing. However, given that end user computing processing is largely indeterminate as to the resources used, this presorting of resource intensive and nonresource intensive set-at-a-time processing is very difficult to do. The resources used by a set-at-a-time process are often unknown until the resource goes into execution, at which point it is too late to separate different end user requests.

Record-at-a-time processing is then necessary for the achievement of performance in the face of much processing. Record-at-a-time processing requires that data be navigated, calculated, manipulated, and so on, one record-at-a-time. This implies much more coding and logic and is inherently unproductive if the speed of coding is the primary measure of productivity. However, record-at-a-time processing is a prerequisite to good performance, as has been discussed. If the end user is operating in an environment where performance is required (i.e., those environments that handle large amounts of data, large amounts of processing, and require good performance and availability), then productivity in that environment *first* requires that performance criteria be met, thus precluding the usage of set-at-a-time processing.

SUMMARY

Despite the fact that the origins of end user computing are found in traditional DP computing, there are many fundamental differences between end user computing and traditional DP:

Types of processing.

Level of detail and data usage.

Intent of processing.

Who actually does processing.

"Truth" and dual data base environments

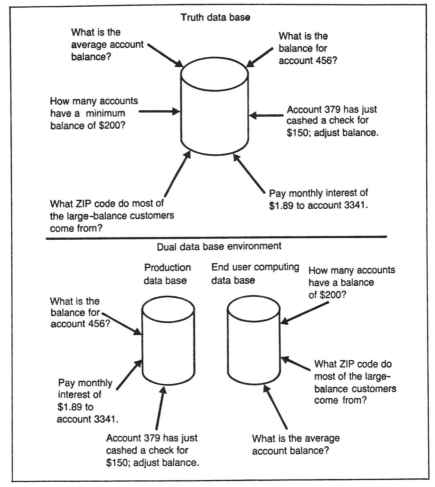

The differences between end user computing and traditional DP are so deep and many that the two types of processing can be considered to be two different modes of operation. The data that serves the different modes of operation can be classified as "truth" data or "dual" data. Truth data—a single source of data for both modes of operation—has an intellectual appeal but works in practice for small amounts of data and small amounts of processing. For larger amounts of data and larger amounts of processing, it is necessary to split data into "dual" data bases.

The differences in the modes of operation do not end with data. The differences extend to data usage. Generally end user software access data one set at a time, and DP accesses data one record at a time. The issue of access has definite productivity and performance implications. Finally, the end user is entering an era of evolution, much like the evolution experienced by the traditional DP organization.

DIRECTIVES AND DIRECTIONS

- End user computing is in a state of evolution today, going through its own unique phases.
- The end user computing evolution will parallel, but not be identical to, the evolution experienced by the data processing organization.
- To achieve maturity, the end user *must* assume full budgetary responsibility for all expenditures.
- There are appropriate and inappropriate uses of the tools of end user computing. The trade-off comes in the flexibility of end user tools and the resources consumed by the tools.
- The effective end user computing environment has as its basis an architecture. One of the foundations of this architecture is a hardware and software "standard operating environment."
- The intent of end user computing is the effective usage of the computer. The classical intent of the data processing usage of the computer is for efficiency of processing.
- End user computing does not require a stringent requirements-gathering exercise, as does the data processing environment, because of the ability to quickly reiterate an end user computing system design.
- The effective end user computing environment focuses on data. When the proper data is available, the end user has many options. When the proper data is not available, the end user is constrained.
- The differences between end user computing and traditional data processing are so great that each forms what can be termed its own "mode of operation."

- There are two schools of thought on data shared between the end user computers and data processing. One school holds that a single "truth" data base is the proper basis. The other school holds that there are so many differences between the environments that each environment requires its own data. This approach can be termed the "dual data base" environment.
- The user friendly software that forms the basis of most end user computing is shaped around access of records of data set-at-a-time. The set-at-a-time processing has its own inherent performance limitations.

The Physical Environment

• •

The first step in establishing an effective end user computer architecture is to address the hardware and software on which end user computing runs. There is a fine balance to be walked—on the one hand, end users should not have their autonomy of processing preempted; on the other hand, a certain amount of discipline in the selection, acquisition, and installation of end user equipment makes sense.

A typical strategy is to establish what can be termed a "standard operating environment." The hardware and software are categorically selected for the entire organization to meet a broad range of needs. The end user is free to choose among the different variations and combinations of choices that are available in the standard operating environment. A certain amount of uniformity of end user computer processing can be achieved at the hardware/software level. As such, the standard operating environment becomes one of the cornerstones of the end user computing architecture.

The hardware and software that support the end user computing environment play an important role because they determine many of the capabilities of the end user:

How much data can the end user process?

How quickly can the end user achieve results?

What communications are possible with other end users?

How easily can the end user make changes?

Can more than one end user share/compare data with another end user?

Such issues are fundamentally tied to or otherwise limited by the hardware and software on which the end user processes data.

END USER HARDWARE

End user computing is generally accomplished on either a mainframe or a personal computer (i.e., either a large processor or a small processor). In the case of departmental end user computing, a mini computer may be used. But by and large, it is normal to find end user computing done on either extreme of the size of processors that are available.

The first efforts of end user computing were on a mainframe in a time-sharing mode of operation. Because of the pioneering efforts, mainframe end user computing maintains momentum today.

When the end user processes on a mainframe, the most common organization of the computer is the division of the mainframe into separate partitions, or "address spaces." Each end user "owns" a unique partition. The end user allocates (or brings active) his or her partition on the mainframe and is then ready to begin processing. The larger the partition, the more power the end user can bring to bear on his or her processing. Each partition is dedicated to a user as shown in Figure 2–1. This mode of operation in the mainframe environment is commonly called the "information center" mode.

Figure 2–1 shows that data is owned by the end user individually while the end user is actively using his or her partition. In addition, the figure shows that all users share a common copy of the data base management system—DBMS. Sharing a common copy of the DBMS means that more processing space (i.e., larger partitions) is available for more users. But if much work is being done simultaneously by many end users from different partitions, the commonly shared DBMS may turn into a bottleneck.

F I G U R E   2-1

Common Configuration of a Mainframe Used for End
User Computing

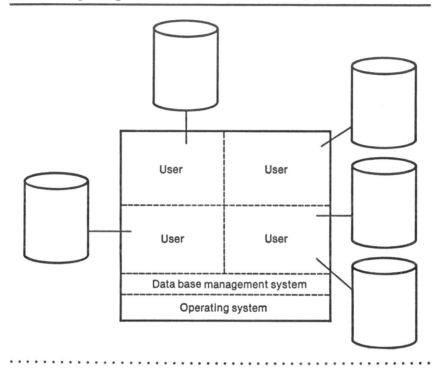

Another common mainframe organization for end user computing is shown by Figure 2-2, wherein part of the standard DBMS code exists in every user's partition. Comparing Figure 2-1 with Figure 2-2 makes it clear that the more commonality of DBMS code there is, the more processing power is available to the community of end users sharing the mainframe processor. When each end user must have a copy of some or all of the DBMS in his or her partition, there is less total operating space available. But the trade-off for the operating space is the capability of each end user actively using a partition to operate independently from other end users active at the same time.

Configuration in which Some of the DBMS Code Exists
Separately for Each User

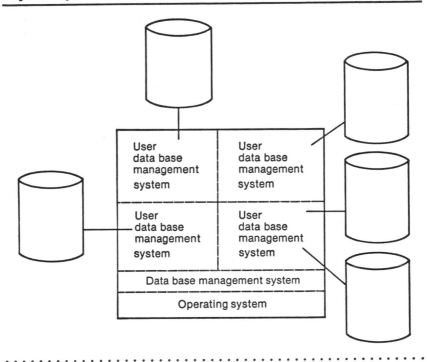

"Ownership of Data"

In both Figure 2–1 and Figure 2–2, data is "owned" by an end
user once the data is allocated to the end user's partition. No
other end user can access the data as long as the data is privately
allocated and controlled by the first end user who lays claim to
the data. Ownership of data is convenient for an end user doing
massive data base scans or updates, but such an arrangement
can inhibit the throughput of the system. Suppose user A has allocated a data base, but user B needs the data base to complete
processing. In this case user B can complete his or her work no
faster than the processing of user A, since user B must wait until user A relinquishes control of the data. One solution to this

conflict is to allow data to be shared among active end user partitions, as shown by Figure 2–3.

The sharing of data is accomplished through the facility of the DBMS code that is common to and controls all active end users. One disadvantage to the sharing of data among active end users is the overhead required to control the common access and usage of data. This overhead (for the protection of the "integrity" of data) may result in system degradation when there are many end users and/or much shared data processing that is occurring.

In the mainframe environment, the end user initiates his or her processing by requesting an active partition in which to operate. If there are no partitions available, the end user must wait. Once a partition is available, it is assigned to the end user,

Shared and Private DBMS

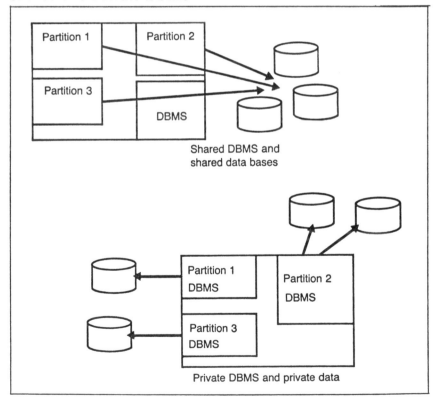

Configuration in which More than One End User at a Time Can Share Data

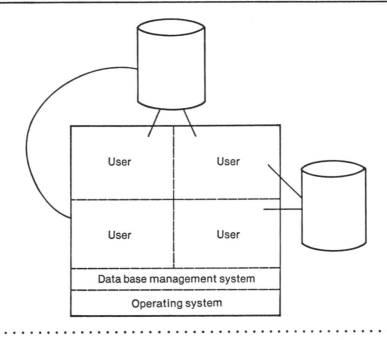

who then commences activities. There are essentially two kinds of activities undertaken by the end user—foreground activities and background activities. Foreground activities are those that are brought to the immediate attention of the user, such as the entry of data, the specification of an end user procedure, and so forth. The responsiveness of the computer is very quick in the processing of foreground activities.

The background activities are those that the end user initiates when there are no immediate needs for the processing to be completed. Typical background might include the copying of a file, the merging or sorting of two or more files, and the relational joining of two data bases. In general, background activities involve massive amounts of computer processing resources, whereas foreground activities involve relatively small amounts of processing.

In some cases the end user does not actively have to be using his or her partition to execute background processing. In this case the end user activates the partition, initiates the background activity (which is queued with other background processing), then releases the partition.

Later the end user reinitiates the partition, and the results of the background (which by this time has already executed) processing are made available. When finished processing, the end user terminates processing, which releases the partition for processing by another user. Then the data that has been activated by the end user is free for allocation by some other end user.

These are some of the major issues of end user computing in the mainframe environment:

What exclusive allocation of data is required, especially for "popular" data?

How many end users will need partitions?

What size of partitions will be needed?

How much system overhead does each partition require?

How long will each end user need to have the partition active?

Is there a peak period when all end users will want to be active?

Can foreground and background processing be easily separated?

End User Mainframe Processing— Advantages/Disadvantages

The early origins of end user computing were in mainframe processing in the "time sharing" mode. Some of the advantages of mainframe end user computing are:

The ability to handle much data. In some cases the volume of data to be manipulated is such that the mainframe *must* be used (as is often the case in actuarial processing for example).

The ability to do large amounts of processing and/or calculation. In this case, the volume of processing, not the volume of data, dictates that end user computing be done on a mainframe.

The ability to pass data from one user to the next. In the mainframe environment, when a user is finished with a data base that has been privately allocated, the end user merely deallocates the data. The data base then joins the pool of data bases available to the mainframe so that some other end user can allocate and use the data base. The net effect is that one mainframe end user can easily "pass" the data to another through the mechanism of allocation/deallocation.

The ability to initiate background processing. In background processing the end user initiates a process to be run later. The user then deactivates the partition. The work initiated by the end user is executed when enough machine resources are available. At a later time, the end user reactivates a partition to find that the work previously initiated is now complete.

Availability of a "system library." Through the facility of the controlling operating system or DBMS software, it is possible to create, store, and access commonly used routines that are available to all end users on the mainframe.

User communication. The communication from one active end user to another is a simple matter. The operating system merely routes the message from the sending end user to the receiving end user. No extra network capabilities are required. In the case where an active user wishes to send a message to an inactive user, the system stores the message until the inactive user becomes active.

Software, application availability. Because of the length of time end user computing has been available on the mainframe and because of the widespread usage at this level, there is an existing body of software from which the end user can choose.

The advantages of the mainframe for end user computing are considerable. There are some major disadvantages, however:

Costs. Compared with processing on the personal computer, mainframe processing costs are relatively expensive.

Peak period congestion. During the prime processing hours, the mainframe may degrade in terms of responsiveness due to the total amount of activity going on in the processor.

Lack of ownership of data. Given the needs of most end users, there is no need for actual physical ownership and possession of data. However, on occasion there is such a need, perceived or otherwise. In this case the storage of data on the mainframe may not be suitable.

System dependence. The ability to use the mainframe processor depends on the availability of the mainframe system—its hardware, software, network, and so forth. When any of these components fail, the result is general system unavailability.

Network and system accessibility. To use the mainframe requires access to the mainframe, through a network. An end user who is unable to access the network cannot do end user computing.

There are then a corresponding set of disadvantages to end user computing on a mainframe. These disadvantages can be succinctly stated as cost and convenience.

END USER COMPUTING ON THE PC

The end user can do the same activities on the PC that can be done on the mainframe. The access of data, manipulation of data, calculation, sorting, formatting of output, printing and storing of results, programming, and so forth, are the kinds of activities that can be done on the PC. From a functionality perspective, there is practically no difference between the end user's usage of the PC and the end user's perspective of the world *after* the end user has allocated data and a partition in the mainframe environment.

The essence of end user computing is autonomy of processing. End user computing, unlike its progenitor—operational processing—is aimed at individual needs and processing. The privacy of end user computing is very much reinforced by the privacy that is possible in using the personal computer. From a hardware perspective, the personal computer is optimal for privacy. Thus the autonomy of end user computing naturally gravi-tates to a processor whose intent is that of individualized needs, that is, the personal computer.

As in the case of mainframe processing, there are advan-tages and disadvantages to end user computing on the micro-processor. Some of the advantages are:

Costs. End user computing on the PC is relatively inexpensive.

Control. The end user has complete control—physical and oth-erwise over the PC. This implies control of data, program, and hardware.

Some of the disadvantages of the PC processing of end user computing are:

Newness of the technology. The PC is a relatively new technol-ogy. As such it is not fully evolved to a mature state, and some of the existing technology is undoubtedly not "bug" free.

Less power, less capacity. Some end user processing cannot sim-ply be run on a personal computer, given the speed of process-ing, available memory, communications links, and so forth.

Less software. Compared with mainframe end user computing, there is significantly less software, both utilitarian and appli-cation.

Limitations on the amount of data handled. Because of memory sizes, transportation of data to and from the PC, and so forth, the amount of data to be manipulated becomes a constraint.

Fewer communication capabilities, especially for unnetworked PCs. The crude method of exchanging floppy disks must suffice for the transferring of data in the face of unnetworked PCs.

End user computing is done in two basic modes—the stan-dalone mode and the networked mode. In the standalone mode, there are no electronic communications with other processors. In the networked mode, there are several possibilities for elec-tronic networking.

NETWORKING PCs

To unlock the full potential of PC processing in the end user computing environment, it is necessary to consider the networking of PCs, which allows the PCs to communicate elec-

F   I   G   U   R   E   2-4

Four Basic Types of Communication Links in Networking PCs

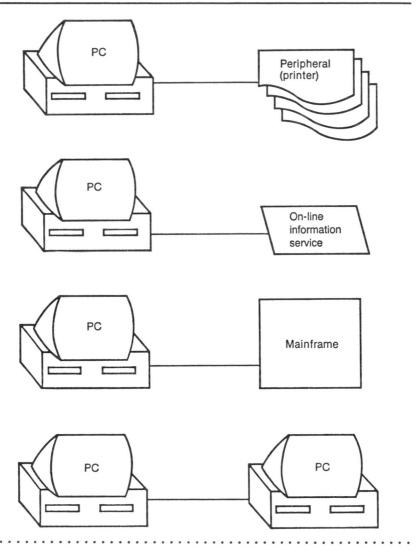

tronically. Data can be shared, messages may be passed, and so forth. There are basically four types of communications links possible (see Figure 2–4):

PC to peripheral link—to printers, storage, and so on.

PC to online information services—to stock quotes, catalogs, data banks, and so on.

PC to mainframe—between the PC and the mainframe.

PC to PC—usually connected by modems or through a local area network (a "lan").

PC-to-PC Connection

When the PC-to-PC connection is made, it can be made either synchronously or asynchronously. A synchronous PC-to-PC connection is one wherein all users in the conversation are actively using the PC. An asynchronous connection is one wherein one or more parties in the communication are not actively using the PC. Figure 2–5 depicts synchronous and asynchronous PC communications. The linkage between PCs can be made through direct wire connectors, lans, and PBXs. Figure 2–6 illustrates the basic linkages that are possible.

The direct connection is fairly straightforward. The local area network connection can be subclassified into three physical topologies: ring, star, and bus. A PBX can be considered, in the broadest terms, to be a degenerate form of a star lan topology. Both lans and PBXs can connect much more than PCs to PCs. They can also connect PCs to printers, storage devices, larger processors, and other lans. Both lans and PBXs are intended (or are at least practical and economical) for short-distance communications.

PHYSICAL LAN TOPOLOGIES

The ring topology is typified by logic that entails "token" passing. The PCs are organized in a ring, wherein each PC receives data from one PC and passes data to another PC. A "token" is passed from one PC to the next, indicating the opportunity to send or receive transmissions. A ring topology is suited to PCs

F   I   G   U   R   E   2-5

Synchronous and Asynchronous PC Communication

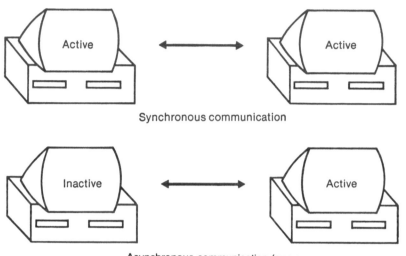

Synchronous communication

Asynchronous communication (one or
more parties may be inactive)

that are physically located closely together, such as might occur
for a department located on a single floor of a building. Rings
depend on the availability of every node for successful operation (in other words, if any node fails, the network fails).

A star topology is a topology in which message trafficking is
administered centrally. The routing of messages is done by a
central controller. In terms of availability, a star topology is both
more flexible and more vulnerable than a ring topology. If any
node becomes unavailable in a star topology, the entire network
does not cease operation. But if the central controller becomes
unavailable, then the network goes down.

A bus topology is generally not suited for small physical environments, like a ring or star topology might be. In general,
there is a higher cost per connection than for either a ring or
star topology. In the case where other topologies must be linked
together, the bus topology serves well as a foundation for con-
necting the different topologies. In terms of reliability, the network is available as long as the bus itself doesn't malfunction.

Three Basic Linkages between PCs

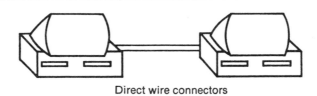

Direct wire connectors

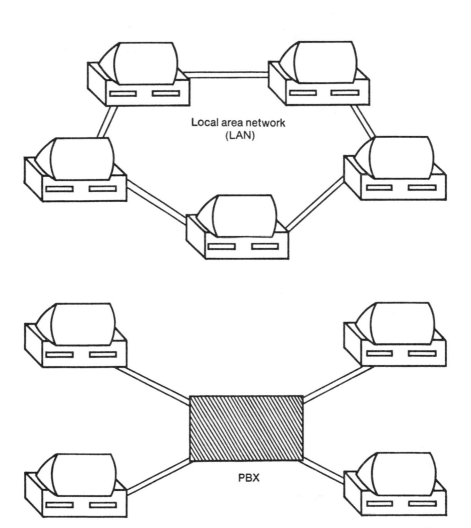

Local area network
(LAN)

PBX

LANs: Three Common Physical Topologies

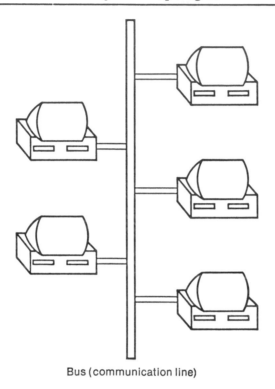

Bus (communication line)

When any given node becomes unavailable, there is no affect on the general unavailability of the network. Figure 2–7 illustrates the different topologies.

TRANSMISSION METHODS

Whatever topology is chosen, there are two basic logical transmission methods—baseband and broadband. Baseband transmits a single message flow, and broadband transmits multiple message flows. The method of transmission correlates to the speed of transmission that is possible, usually measured in bits/second. Figure 2–8 illustrates the basic differences between baseband and broadband.

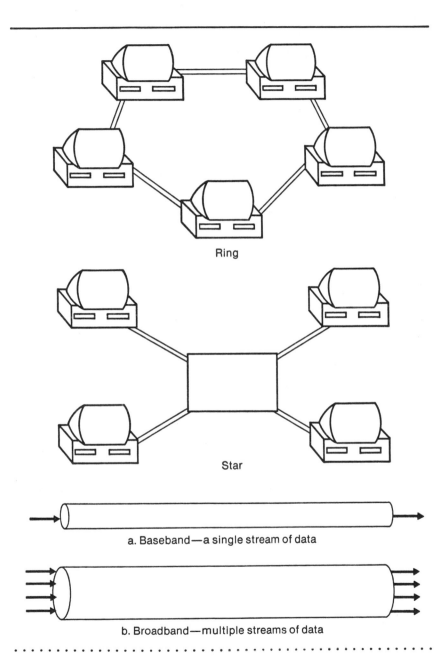

Ring

Star

a. Baseband—a single stream of data

b. Broadband—multiple streams of data

In general, baseband can be considered a dedicated transmission medium, and broadband can be considered a multiple-channel transmission medium. The relative speeds of transmission for baseband are roughly 10 to 1, with baseband transmitting about 1/10 of the rate of broadband. As a rule, baseband is less expensive than broadband, and baseband is generally used for much shorter distances.

Physical Media

There are three physical media generally used for transmission of data communications. These media are twisted pair wire, coaxial cable, and fiber optics. Twisted pair wiring is used for baseband transmission; coaxial cable is used for either baseband or broadband; and fiber optics is used for broadband transmission.

MAINFRAME/PC LINK

The mainframe/PC linkage can be made with either a modem or a coaxial cable if the PC is located near enough to the mainframe. Transmission between mainframe and the PC is slow when a modem is used. When coaxial cable is used, transmission speeds of 9,600 bits per second are possible.

In general when a PC is used to communicate with a mainframe, the PC must emulate a terminal with which the mainframe normally communicates. To accomplish this a terminal emulation board is installed in the PC, which causes the mainframe to react as if it is communicating with a dedicated terminal.

An integral part of the PC/mainframe link is the software that is used to transfer data to and from the PC. Most software packages operate in this mode under the control of a larger piece of software. For example, CCA's Model 204 has software capabilities for downloading data on a PC that is likewise operating under the control of CCA's software. Some of the capabilities include mainframe data selection, summarization, and sorting of data prior to download to the PC.

The issues of end user computing and the microprocessor revolve around the physical limitations of the microprocessor. The availability of software, transportation and usage of data

End User/Decision Support Processing in the
Micro/Mainframe Environment

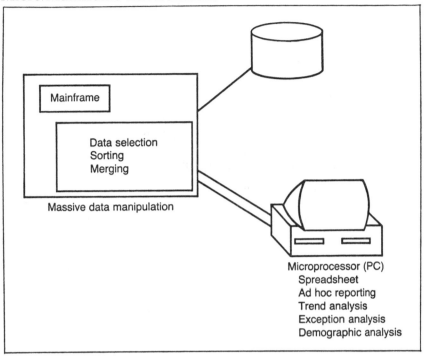

Mainframe

Data selection
Sorting
Merging

Massive data manipulation

Microprocessor (PC)
Spreadsheet
Ad hoc reporting
Trend analysis
Exception analysis
Demographic analysis

outside the microprocessor, and limitations on the amount of
data that can be handled are all issues germane to the end user.

End User Computing in the Mixed
Mainframe/Micro Environment

A third possibility for end user computing is the usage of both a
mainframe (or other large-scale processor) and a microprocessor. This mixed environment presents the end user with many
possibilities. In some ways this combination offers the best of
both worlds.

Where there are massive amounts of data that the end user
can store, sort, merge, and so on, the data may be housed and
manipulated on the mainframe. But where there is spreadsheet
processing, "what if" analysis, trend analysis, and so on, there

is no need to use the expensive machine cycles of the mainframe. In short, in a well-planned environment, the mainframe and the microprocessor can be used to complement each other.

Integration Issues

The issues of hardware/software integration over the end user computing environment are the same whether the operational/end user computing environment is characterized by a mainframe/micro, micro/micro, or mainframe/mainframe orientation. Only the specifics of the issues change as the configurations themselves change.

The two primary issues of hardware integration are compatibility and capacity. The issues of compatibility refer to the ability of data to be passed effectively and efficiently to and from the different processing nodes of the end user computing environment and from the operational environment to the end user computing environment. In general, data is passed to the end user computing environment from the data processing environment, and transactions are passed the reverse direction. This trafficking arrangement implies that the vast amount of traffic flows from the data processing environment to the end user computing environment.

The second compatibility issue revolves around the flow of data from one end user computing node to another node. At this level data is fairly refined, so the total volume of traffic is usually not an issue. However, the meaning of the data, the refinement of the data, the interpretation of the data—although not strictly hardware compatibility issues—loom as obstacles to the effective sharing of data in end user computing when two or more end users share data.

It is easy to say that a protocol converter can allow any two nodes in the end user computing network to communicate. Although protocol conversion is necessarily a part of the interface between two otherwise incompatible nodes, there are other issues of compatibility:

How efficient is the conversion?

Is data from the sending node sometimes uninterpretable to the receiving node?

Are all forms of data meaningful to the receiving node able to be expressed?

Capacity Issues

The second major hardware integration issue is that of capacity, both in the processing nodes and in the network itself. In the ideal case, any processing node can be expanded to meet the needs of the user at that node. But such is often not the case. The characteristics of systems greatly change in the face of volumes of data and volumes of processing, and end user computing is no exception to this rule. As processing needs expand, the end user would like simple hardware expansions to meet processing needs. Having to change basic architectures is no more palatable to the end user whether the end user is operating on a mainframe or a micro. For this reason, the hardware planner (or end user, or whoever is purchasing hardware) is safest acquiring the smallest processor in a line of compatible processors that will meet the end user's needs. Come the day that more processing power is necessary, the end user can simply upgrade processors.

In line with that same philosophy, it is an observable fact that the end user usually fills up whatever capacity is allocated. To control the hardware budget, the planner does best to start off with the smallest processor that suffices and then carefully move to larger processors as justified.

Hardware Planning

The previous discussions of hardware compatibility serve to highlight the need for a corporate end user computing hardware plan as an essential part of the architecture for the end user computing environment. It is easy to envision the chaos that can result when end users "do their own thing" (and it should be remembered that the essence of end user computing is autonomy of processing). But the processing done by the end user still should be done within the confines of a common framework, which certainly includes (but is not limited to) hardware and software.

A certain synergy can be attained when there is a degree of uniformity of processing across environments. Users can exchange information, transfer skills, consolidate training and purchases, and so forth when there is a standard environment for the community of end users. The hardware part of the architecture should address (at a minimum):

Flow of data going into the end user computing environment.

Volume of processing done by end users.

Nature of processing of end user computing.

Degree of summarization and/or other data refinement in end user computing.

Discipline of hardware acquisition is one of the keys to the achievement of an effective end user computing architecture, but it is worthwhile to note that it is only one of the necessary conditions to the achievement of the architecture.

END USER COMPUTING SOFTWARE

The second major component of the end user computing architecture is software. A hardware strategy is necessary, but a hardware strategy alone is inadequate. The next necessary component of the architecture is the software that the end user operates. In many ways the software drives the hardware decisions.

A common type of software for the end user computing environment is called the fourth-generation language, or 4GL. A 4GL is a language that is geared for manipulation by the end user. In general, 4GLs are optimized around ease of use and contain such powerful constructs as set-at-a-time processing. They may be changed by the end user interactively, in an unstructured fashion. The selection of the 4GL(s) that a shop will use has far-reaching consequences. The language(s) needs to meet the needs of all end users, some of which are very experienced and some of which are neophytes. Some end users do calculation-intensive processing, and some do input/output record processing. Some end users do financial modeling, and some end users do trend analysis. There is, relatively speaking, little uniformity in the types of processing being done by the end user. Because of the lack of uniformity, it is common to have multiple 4GLs in a company, operating on a variety of machines and serving a variety of functions. But there still needs to be a certain amount of discipline at the software level, despite the diversity of needs.

An Example of a 4GL and Its Output

```
0010  FIND PERSONNEL WITH STATE = 'TX' AND CITY = 'EL PASO'
      OR = 'DALLAS'
0020  SORTED BY CITY NAME
0030  ACCEPT IF SEX = 'F'
0040  DISPLAY NAME,FIRST-NAME,CITY,SALARY
0050  AT BREAK OF CITY DO SKIP 1 WRITE
0060     'TOTAL SALARIES': OLD(CITY) T*SALARY SUM(SALARY)
0070     SKIP 1 DOEND
0080  AT END OF DATA DO SKIP 1 WRITE
0090     'AVERAGE SALARY': AVER(SALARY) / 'MINIMUM SALARY':
         MIN(SALARY) /
0100     'MAXIMUM SALARY': MAX(SALARY) DOEND END
```

PAGE 1   86-05-26 16:27:37

LAST-NAME	FIRST-NAME	HOME-CITY	FIXED SALARY
Jensen	Lolly	Dallas	9907
Kokomo	Britt	Dallas	10900
Silverman	Kay Ann	Dallas	7806
Total Salaries: Dallas			28613
Aanonsen	Gloria	El Paso	8600
Curry	Barbara	El Paso	9608
Curry	Kathy	El Paso	8005
Picken	Jenny	El Paso	11089
Vance	Robin	El Paso	9007
Total Salaries: El Paso			46309

Average Salary: 10703
Minimum Salary: 7806
Maximum Salary: 11089

Another common type of end user software is the spreadsheet. The spreadsheet in many ways represents the ultimate in end user autonomy. One is as unconstrained in the usage of the spreadsheet as one would be sitting in front of a blank sheet of paper. In a short amount of time, the user can create a large model whose calculations and transformations of data are done accurately and automatically. Issues that relate to the different software that is typically found in the end user computing environment are:

Processing transportability across machines. Given the growth in the amount and diversity of processing that end users experience, it is likely that they will outgrow whatever processor they first work on and will transport existing systems onto another processor at some point. Some software is transportable, and some isn't. (This issue is not as important in the end user computing environment as it is in the traditional DP environment.) In the end user computing environment, some types of systems are written, used, and discarded. For these systems, once they have reached a state of maturity, transportability is not a large issue.

Sharing, transportation of data. If one end user wishes to share results with another and wishes the results to be passed electronically, the data flow between end users is greatly simplified if the two end users are using the same software and hardware. If the same software is not being used, then a conversion must be done, which further complicates the sharing and transportation of data.

Training, support. Each piece of software, however autonomous it is, requires its own training and support. The more software packages a company has, the more overhead is entailed for training and support. The organizational software strategy then, should balance the different sets of end user needs versus the costs of training and support.

Ability to serve a variety of needs and to grow. Even for processing that is functionally similar, there is a need to serve a variety of end users. Some end users have been doing their own processing for a long time; some are just beginning. Some end users want to explore the details of their processing; some just want to get the job done. Some users want to manipulate massive amounts of data; some want to do large calculations. End user computing software should be able to service a wide variety of needs within the normal confines of the software.

Resource utilization. The flexibility of end user software comes at a price—the hardware required to run the software on. End user computing software is not known for its efficiency. Although the primary intent of end user computing is the ability to quickly build and change systems, there must be an awareness of the resources consumed. For those users that do not pay attention to hardware costs on the theory that hardware is getting cheaper all the time, there is a rude awakening when it is discovered that end user software can consume resources at a faster rate than the resources drop in price.

License costs. Generally, licensing costs are the least concern of the person selecting packages. But, in some environments, such as the microprocessor environment, when the license cost is multiplied times the number of users, the cost can be considerable. The vendor's pricing structure then becomes an issue.

Extendibility, development prospects for the software. Some software has a very limited range of capabilities. Other software seems to extend into many areas. The prospects for extension become a long-term issue when considering a package as a candidate for selection in the standard operating environment.

Functionality. Does the software extend the capabilities and possibilities of the end user? Software that is effective serves to automate, document, or standardize the tasks the end user does.

SELECTING END USER COMPUTING SOFTWARE

Knowing the basic issues for end user computing software leads to the criteria for establishing a standard operating environment. The following (rather generic) list of specific criteria is a direct result of the major issues facing the end user.

Some Criteria for End User Computing Software

In support of these desired functions, a list of criteria for end user computing software might include the following data definition features:

- Physical attributes handled—

  Alphanumeric.
  Integer.
  Floating point.
  Binary.
  Packed decimal.
  Logical.

- Dictionary attributes handled—

  Element structures.
  Synonyms.
  Data relationships.
  Key identification.
  Foreign key identification.
  Field name limitations (length of field).
  Data element commands.
  Total number of field names handled.
  Interactive access to the dictionary.
  End user computing/operational dictionary interface.

- Logical data base structure capabilities—

  Physical/logical separation.
  Subset/superset views of data.
  Resequencing capabilities.
  Relational join capabilities.

- Reporting features—

    Interactive screen preparation.

    Default reporting.

    Page break.

    Minimal report requests (i.e., simple listing).

    Summarization, subtotal facility.

    Reformatting, default overrides.

    Destination control (printer, screen, other).

    Report size limitation and control.

- Record selection control—

    Set-at-a-time processing.

    Record subset comparison.

    Standard comparison, manipulation operators (equal, less than, greater than, etc.).

    Numeric, alphanumeric comparison.

    Range comparison.

    Substring comparison.

    Boolean expression (AND, OR, etc.).

    Cross-structural comparisons (i.e., criteria for selection at different levels or types of data).

    Summary within selected class of data (average, total, etc.).

    Mathematical operations within selection criteria.

    Ability to easily (parametrically) change selection/calculation criteria.

    Default/override values for number of records selected/compared.

- Temporary field manipulation—

    Limited restrictions on the naming, usage of temporary field.

Default/override for display format of temporary field.

Cross temporary field referencibility.

Recursive temporary field referencibility.

Ability to use mathematical and logical operators with temporary field.

Standard language conventions used in conjunction with temporary fields.

Display of temporary fields.

- Language functions—

Mathematical, logical operators.

Stand mathematical precedence of operators.

Exits for user-created functions.

Date calculations/manipulations.

"Macro" capability.

- String operations—

Concatenation.

Truncation.

Alpha/numeric, numeric/alpha conversion.

Substring operations.

Standard string modification, formatting.

Tabled encoding, decoding.

- Conditional processing—

Ability to use relational operators.

AND/OR usage.

Matching substring comparison.

Nesting of logic capabilities.

Ability to define a temporary field for use in record selection.

Closeness operators (as opposed to matching operators).

- Data formatting—

    Comma in numeric values.
    Zero truncation.
    Rounding.
    Decimal specification.
    Fill character specification.
    Printed field length of display.
    Character masking.
    Default column width (overrides as well).
    Horizontal spacing control.
    Heading control.
    Total/subtotal control.
    Printing suppression on matching value.
    Margin setting.
    Page number control.
    Underline control by column.
    Page break control.
    Page number reset.

- Graphics—

    Pie chart capability.
    Bar chart comparisons.
    Graphing capability.
    Lettering, heading control.

- Statistical capabilities—

    Regression analysis.
    Variance analysis.
    Correlations.
    Exponential smoothing.
    Discriminant analysis.

Factor analysis.

Descriptive statistics.

Time-series variability.

Cross tabs, hash totals.

- Productivity—

    Data dictionary access, generation of code.

    Menu generation.

    Screen largest generation, manipulation.

    Common error routines, common calculation routines.

    Data validation routines.

    Data base definition, allocation.

    Cross-referencing of usage, occurrences of data.

    Report generation, default processing.

    Set and record processing, as desired.

    Online editing.

    Program skeleton generation.

    Minimal programming skills required.

    Online "HELP" available.

    Nonnavigational access.

    Simple display facility.

    Parameters used with cataloged procedures.

    Cataloged procedures.

- Capacity parameters/limitations—

    Maximum number of fields.

    Maximum number of record types.

    Linkage limitations to/from mainframe.

    Physical data base size.

    Linkage limitations to/from PC to PC.

Active fields per request.

Reentrant code.

Active temporary fields per request.

Required memory.

Library files.

Operating system.

Processor utilization.

- Client costs—

    Initial acquisition.

    Ongoing maintenance.

    Technical support required.

- Mainframe/micro linkage—

    Download of data.

    Transaction upload.

    Software support.

    PC controlled mainframe selection of data.

    Refinement, selection prior to transmission.

    Mainframe/PC language compatibility.

    General interface capability such as COBOL, IMS, and Lotus 1–2–3.

Other general criteria for end user computing software selection include:

Financial modeling.

Application package availability.

Available utilities (sorts, merger, etc.).

Procedural language capabilities, interfaces.

Vendor responsiveness.

All of the facilities and features in the criteria list may or may not be found in a single package. Even among packages that do have most or all of these features, there most likely will be differences in features, strengths, weaknesses, and even additional features.

The selection of software for the standard operating environment then usually comes down to a weighting process, in which each of the features is independently ranked according to its perceived usefulness to the organization. Then the qualifying software packages are rated item by item, and the weight of each item is factored to produce a proper choice.

The usual approach to the end user computing dilemma of needing to see data summarized and shaped in many different fashions is to create multiple copies of the data. The "dual data base" approach is especially appropriate in light of large volumes of data and/or processing. But the dual data base approach does not necessarily imply a dual data base management system. Indeed, there are many advantages to having a single data base management system that can handle *both* operational and decision support needs.

When there is a single data base management system, there is a marked need for fewer technical support personnel. In addition, the skills that must be learned throughout the shop are simplified. There is no need to learn one set of development skills for operational systems and another set for DSS systems. And there are other economics of consolidation that can be enjoyed when there is a single technology that can serve the dual data base environment.

As an example of a single technology serving dual data base needs, consider the technology of ADR (Applied Data Research). Figure 2–9 shows a hardware configuration with ADR software that might be found in a conventional dual data base environment. Three processors are shown. One (the operational one) is dedicated to doing transaction processing, where there is consistently two to three seconds in response time. Of the software listed beneath this processor, CICS (an IBM product for teleprocessing monitoring) handles the trafficking of messages to and from the mainframe and the terminals that are networked to the mainframe. CICS service allows application

Dual Data Base Environment Serviced by a Single Technology:
ADR's DATACOM/DB

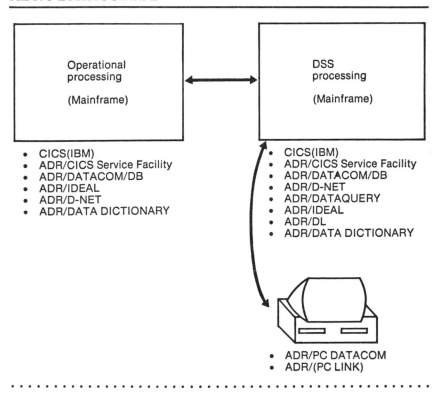

programs written for CICS to issue data base requests and provides a method of controlling the data base resources available to CICS transactions. ADR/DATACOM/DB is the actual data base management system that services the data base activities. ADR/IDEAL is the fourth-generation language that is used to access DATACOM/DB. And ADR/D–NET is the networking software that allows data to be shared across multiple computer systems in a network.

The other mainframe processor is used for development and decision support processing. This processor does much batch processing, such as data base scans, merges, sorts, and summarizations. The software found on this machine is shown below the processor. ADR/DATAQUERY is a software product for end users to directly access their decision support data. ADR/DL is the software product that produces COBOL-like code for nonend users' data requests.

The third processor shown is a microprocessor intended for individual end user computing processing. There is only one piece of software shown: ADR/PC DATACOM. This software allows data to be selected and manipulated on the PC. A major component of ADR/PC DATACOM is ADR/PC LINK, the mechanism by which data is transported to and from the micro to the mainframe. There might also be found other pieces of software on the PC, such as LOTUS 1–2–3 or other spreadsheet applications.

Even though multiple pieces of software are required because of the diversity of functions that must be accomplished, the environment is still integrated in the sense that there is a single technological approach. Consider a dual data base architecture implemented under an unintegrated approach. Such problems as incompatibility of data, inability to transfer data, and inability to define data under a common dictionary all greatly complicate the implementation and effectiveness of the dual data base environment.

Architectural compatibility at the technological level is one of the foundations of the effective end user computing environment. Another level of architectural discipline required—at the data architecture level—will be discussed in Chapter 6.

INSTALLATION GUIDE FOR END USER COMPUTING

Once the standard operating environment has been established (which includes both hardware and software), the next step is to plan the creation and implementation of the end user environment. In some cases the environment will be partially in place. In other cases existing equipment will not fit with the standard operating environment. There must be resolution as to how to identify and handle nonstandard equipment.

After the planning of implementation, comes the plan for installation. Installing end user computing equipment requires special consideration, if for no other reason than end user computing hardware is often the very first piece of equipment of its kind, with its own peculiar needs, that the end user has ever installed or used. It is highly likely that the end user is unprepared for the advance planning and preparation that is required for installation.

Number of Offices

In some cases the number of offices to be installed is easily determined; in some cases it isn't. The number of offices to be installed critically affects the whole scope of the installation effort, so a finite number of offices must be established at least as a target. Failing a solid definition of the number of offices to be installed, a backup strategy should account for the numerous permutations of offices that can be installed. For example, a hotel chain is preparing to install an end user computing system for hotels of more than 350 rooms. Hotels having less than 350 rooms can participate on a voluntary basis if local management deems it desirable. The installation schedule, once the basic number of installations is determined (or at least projected), is a function of many variables—the availability of installers, vendor lead time and delivery requirements, and end users' work schedules, and so forth.

The planner must determine the basic number of installations and a schedule for them. A cutoff date should be determined for voluntary participation. The staffing requirements, lead times, delivery dates, training, and so forth can be determined once the preliminary installation schedule has been established. Any requests for participation after the schedule has been established should either be scheduled in a second phase or denied.

Location and Size

If the sites are all in the same general geographic area and of a similar size, many logistic problems can be eliminated. However, geographic concentration is often not the case. Many companies maintain offices countrywide, and the size of the office (and the nature of the work) varies from city to city. Availability of accommodations in the case of large installations, and the staff's willingness to travel can be a major consideration.

Time zone changes can create some unexpected problems. The amount of time required by the installation for direct contact with a head office can be a major consideration. For example, installations on the East Coast with head offices on the West coast may require support staff to be available for phone consultations at East Coast hours, and so forth.

Number of People to Be Trained

Consideration must be given to how many end user computing personnel and the level of sophistication of the end user need to be trained, both on and off site. If a hotline for trouble calls is to be provided, the personnel managing the phones must be trained and put in place before installation.

Follow-up Training

When installation is finished, it may be prudent to schedule an audit of the end user computing site to determine if any additional training is required and to resolve any problems that may have arisen. The audit need not be long or overly involved but will establish good working relations between the end user and support personnel. Too often, end user computing sites feel "dumped on" as far as new systems are concerned, and maintaining an ongoing relationship with support personnel can defuse potentially awkward situations. A by-product of an audit is a user profile, that makes subsequent upgrade or changes in hardware or software easier.

Schedule of Training Classes

Care should be taken not to overschedule training staff and not to overwhelm end user trainees. An organized, well-designed training schedule with adequate support staff in place will do much to aid the smooth transition from no end user computing to the establishment of the end user computing environment.

There is a difference between classes for staff familiar with "computerese," and classes for conversions from manual-to-computerized systems (i.e., for the neophyte). Classes for experienced end users can generally deal with the details and fine points of the new systems, emphasizing such basics as how to turn the terminal on. Classes for manual-to-computerized systems should be scheduled fairly close to the installation date. These classes need to address the basic use of computers. Fear of computers is not fiction in many cases where the neophyte is first exposed to end user computing equipment and systems.

Security

One issue often overlooked in installation and training is security—from security of the data itself to the number of backups required to ensure no data loss in case of hard failure. The number of backup copies of data required by any system depends upon the criticality of the data. Hard files often have a list of date checks built in and require fewer copies than do diskettes. The installed software may provide as part of the package backup routines or tapes of stripped data to use with recovery procedures. If backup routines or tape strips are not provided, these facilities will have to be added. The user must determine the criticality of the data and how much of a loss can be sustained. The type of hardware/software being used will determine how many and what type of backup copies must be made and how long they must be saved.

Many offices have a series of security measures for manual systems already in place. Confidential sensitive files are kept in locked cabinets for example. Access to certain files is restricted, and so on. Very often computerization eliminates these security measures. Care should be taken to build into a system the required level of security. For instance, sensitive data on diskette should be locked away at night. Security codes (that change regularly) should be built into the system to restrict access to sensitive parts of the system and data. Audit procedures should be built into the system to provide an external check of dates and should also validate totals, hash totals, and so on, either manually or by machine.

Figure 2–10 shows a form that can be used to develop a user profile.

Collectively, the user profiles across all installations describe the environment and the requirements for installation. The usefulness of a collective description of an end user computing environment is that such global issues as sharing of data, communications, costs, trends, and changes can be addressed from a corporate perspective. In addition, any given environment is described so that a troubleshooter working remotely has an idea of the physical equipment discussed.

F I G U R E   2–10

Sample Format for a User Profile

```
                              User Profile
    Location: _____
    Size:_____
    Phones: _____Number: _____Extensions: _____
    Number of Personnel: _____
    Key Employee:  _____
    Hardware: Mainframe:_____Terminal type and number:_____
    Software: _____Version: _____Hotline number: _____
    Recovery Procedures: _____
    Security:  _____
    Telecom Info:  Modem type and number:  _____
                   Local phone co.?_____Long distance?_____
    Environment:  Noise level?_____Window placement?_____
                   A/C? _____Heat? _____
    Up Time? _____
    Days Closed? _____
    Any Other Info? _____
                   _____

    Floor Plan:  _____




    Central Office Skill Level:  _____
```

END USER SYSTEM RESPONSIBILITY

One of the great attractions of end user computing is the freedom to build one's own system. This appeal is powerful, especially in light of the widespread user dissatisfaction with data processing's traditional lack of responsiveness in the development of and maintenance of systems. However, with autonomy and freedom comes responsibility—something that most end users give little thought to in the haste to build systems:

Cost justification. The end user is free to purchase whatever gear or software that can be justified. No longer must one rely on someone else's allocation. On the other hand, the end user is solely responsible for the results that ultimately justify the costs.

Physical storage, security. The end user is responsible for the physical presence and security of the equipment. Power sources, building vibration, outside interference, protection of data are now the sole responsibility of the end user.

Data contents. Perhaps most important, the end user is responsible for the analytic results achieved by processing. Data input, data processing, algorithms used, and dispositions of the results are now the responsibility of the end user. When DP supplies raw data on which to operate, it is the end user's responsibility to determine whether or not the data is appropriate, and if not, what is needed. If data is calculated or otherwise derived by the end user and is further stored, the end user is solely responsible for the accuracy, usage, and storage of the data.

Documentation. The end user is responsible for all system and data documentation. This includes being able to explain previous processing, the content and usage of stored data, the interface between two or more systems, the assumptions made during processing, the selection algorithms used in preparing input, and so forth.

Processing specifications. What processing occurred? Can it be audited? Reported? When did the processing occur? Where? What limitations are there? What applicabilities are there?

SUMMARY

The selection of hardware and software is very important for the end user computing environment because its long-term growth and usage is ultimately shaped by the physical systems on which it runs. Although autonomy is the very essence of end user computing, from an architectural standpoint it makes sense to adopt a "standard operating environment" for hardware and software. The standard operating environment creates an environment for synergism, wherein the community of users can grow. The economics to be gained in training, support, quantity discount, and transferability of skills all reinforce the importance of the standard operating environment.

End user computing can run on mainframes and micros. There are advantages and disadvantages to both types of hardware. At the micro level, the most effective use is in a networked mode. Networking can be achieved in a variety of topologies using a variety of physical media. Software from the standard operating environment should focus on technology that can serve a wide level of usages—from the neophyte to the expert, from the analyst to the clerk. Responsibility for care and maintenance, as well as content of analysis shifts to the end user when the control shifts to the end user.

DIRECTIVES AND DIRECTIONS

- The standard operating environment has two components—a hardware and a software component. The standard operating environment is one major component of the architected end user computing environment.
- End user computing can be done either on a large processor (usually a mainframe or a minicomputer) or on a small processor (a microprocessor). Each environment has its own characteristics and strengths and weaknesses.
- The trade-offs between end user computing on a large processor and a small processor revolve around costs and capabilities.
- Certain kinds of end user computing, such as actuarial processing, have to be done on a processor that is large.

- The issues of end user computing on the mainframe center around system throughput, DBMS sharing, partition size, and ownership of data.
- The issues of end user computing on the personal computer center around the physical limitations of the processor, the transportation of data to and from the processor, communications with other processors, the relative costs of computing, and so forth.
- An option in which it is possible to enjoy the best of both worlds is where end user computing is done on both a mainframe and a microprocessor. Such an environment requires a mainframe/microcommunications link and supporting software.

End User Computing and the Organization

• •

The world of end user computing is rapidly advancing on many fronts simultaneously. New technology, new applications, and new capabilities for the end user and decision support processing are growing so rapidly that keeping track of changes is almost impossible. This explosion is felt in many places and in many ways. But perhaps the biggest long-term impact of this explosive change is on the organization itself. The data processing landscape—indeed, the operational organization as well—is changing and will never be the same again. What changes are happening to the organization? What forces are at work? Where is the organization now, and where is it headed?

THE INFORMATION CENTER

The effectiveness of end user computing is optimized when end users directly control their processing. But there are technical entry barriers to the end user's accessing and usage of data. To expedite the end user's acceptance of the available technical tools, a certain amount of assistance and guidance from data processing is provided.

The most common organizational vehicle for end user computing is known as the "information center." The information center is where the end user turns for help in solving technical problems, for guidance in the location of data, for getting started in end user computing, and so forth. The information center is usually staffed by experienced DP personnel who are also adept at directly interfacing with the end user. The information center may be a physical location or may merely be an organizational unit designated by the data processing organization. There may be a single information center for all applications or an individual information center for each application analysis group.

Almost universally the end user organizations embrace the information center environment in the same pattern. First one end user application group forms, then another, and another, and so on. Each group centers around the work being done by a single application and forms independently and quietly, in concert with no other group. Indeed, one of the great appeals of the end user computing environment is the independence it affords. Figure 3–1 depicts the environment after several different application-oriented end user computing groups have formed, each feeding off of a single central system of record (i.e., operational data).

The end user computing groups are aligned primarily by application. For example, in a manufacturing environment, there will be separate end user computing groups for production control, inventory control, bills of material, end user personnel, and so on. Each group has its own programs, data, and operating philosophies and very little contact or coordination with other application-oriented end user computing groups. Each of the end user groups is supplied data primarily from the system of record environment. Once the data leaves the system of record environment, it is controlled entirely by the application-oriented end user computing group.

The result of the separation of application-oriented end user groups is that each group is isolated, with little communication or coordination with other groups. It has been suggested that a technical solution to this isolation might be local area networks (LANs). LANs provide the capability to pass data from one end user processor to the next when the end users are operating on microprocessors. But predictably, the LAN will be used almost exclusively within the application-oriented end user computing group, as shown by Figure 3–2.

Figure 3–2 shows that there is very little communication between application-oriented end user computing groups. The reason is more political and organizational than technical. The

F   I   G   U   R   E   3-1

The End User Computing Environment: Embracing the
Information Center

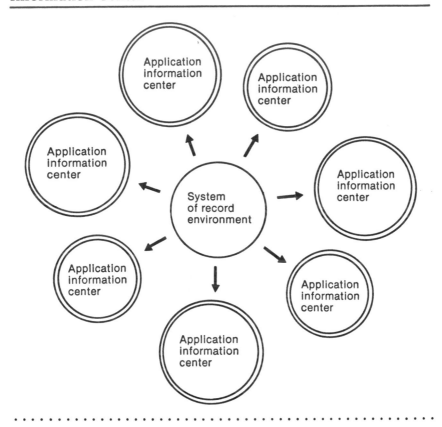

application-oriented groups almost universally have an attitude
of autonomy. User friendliness, micro/mainframe downloads,
fourth-generation languages and the like free the user from the
controls of data processing and, for that matter, any other processing group. The application-oriented groups, in the forma-
tive stages, then see no need for external control.

Each independent end user computing group has its own
data, the origin of which is usually the system of record, as
shown by Figure 3–3. The data that exist in the information center environment (i.e., across all application-oriented end user

F   I   G   U   R   E   3-2

Local Area Networks ("LANs") in the Application Information Center Group

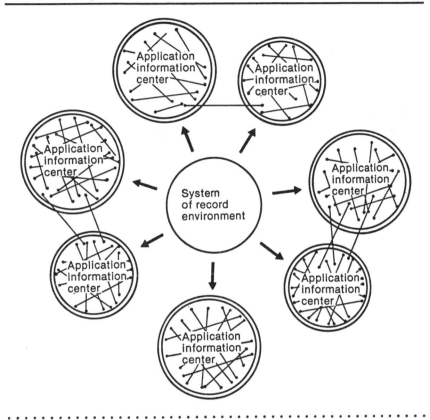

computing groups), then, are redundant, even though the data generally originate from a single nonredundant source, the system of record.

Nonuniform Processing

Because of the autonomy of the groups, the interpretation of the data, the editing, the processing, the selection, the refinement, and so forth are not done uniformly from one group to the next. The result is that the output produced by the different applica-

Data Redundancy among the Different Application
Information Center Groups

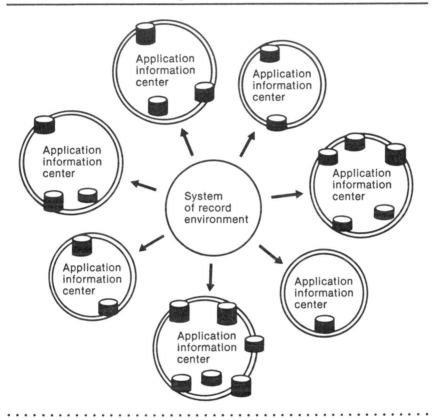

tion-oriented end user computing groups widely varies, even
though the origin of the data was the same.

Consider a hypothetical case. One day the marketing end
user computing group advised management, after much study,
that the number of outlet centers should be increased by 25 percent. The next week the manufacturing end user computing
group advised management to cut inventory and lay off staff.
Both end user computing groups began with the same data but
arrived at diametrically different conclusions because of the
autonomous and inconsistent treatment of the data.

At this time, upper management became dissatisfied with the decision support process because different people, using the same data, arrived at very different conclusions. This difference in results was no trivial matter either, since the long-term direction of the organization was at stake. The problem was not technical, and the decision support managers could not look to data processing to resolve discrepancies. At this point, upper management reached a crucial point in the life of end user computing and the information center concept. One alternative was to abandon end user computing altogether. This would ensure that there would be no major conflicts between different end user computing groups in the future. But this decision would not take advantage of the possibilities of end user computing. Another alternative was to take no action and let nature take its course. Eventually one application-oriented end user computing group would gain credibility at the expense of other groups. A frustrating and unnecessary territorial struggle among the different end user computing groups would commence.

A third approach was to insist on organizational discipline. Instead of allowing internecine warfare, management could actively thrash through the issues underlying the differences in end user computing processing. Eventually some of the autonomy of the individual end user computing groups would disappear. The result would be transformation of the end user computing environment from an undisciplined environment to an architected, disciplined environment.

Management's Past Support

Management's past track record in supporting decision support processing and in not supporting organizational discipline makes it a good bet that the second alternative will occur in most shops—that a struggle for credibility and territory will ensue among the different application-oriented end user computing groups. This inevitably leads to a very unstable (i.e., organizationally unstable) environment, as depicted by Figure 3–4.

Figure 3–4 shows that the insularity of the different end user computing groups will crumble. The posture of insularity and autonomy by the different groups is inherently unstable. De-

F   I   G   U   R   E   3-4

Basic Organization of the Autonomous Application
Information Center Group

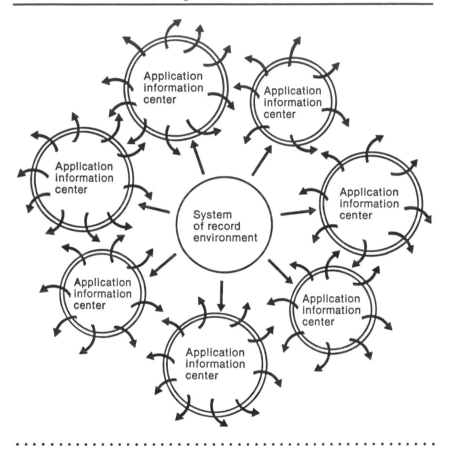

pending upon management's stance, stability will be reached in
one of two ways—either through the winning of territory by a
single application-oriented group or because management dictates a disciplined approach and follows through with the activity and support required to break down the autonomy between
the different groups. The result will be an end user computing
environment where there is a uniform treatment of data and
processing. In short, the end user computing environment

turns into a disciplined, architected environment. Unlike the unstable predecessor, the stable environment will not have uncontrolled, inconsistent redundancy of data and processing. There will still be different end user computing groups for different kinds of functionally disparate processing (a personnel information group, a customer service group, etc.). But different groups in the stable environment will not manipulate functionally common data or processes.

The Stable Information Center Environment

The different relationships between end user computing and business were depicted by Figure 1–7. In the figure the relationships were shown in their most basic form, from the perspective of a single end user. But consider what the relationship looks like from the perspective of the business of the organization and from data processing systems when there are multiple end user computing groups attempting to analyze and direct the corporation, as shown in Figure 3–5.

The messages sent out by such a conglomeration must necessarily be confusing and conflicting, and it is the confusion and conflict that leads to the instability of the unarchitected end user computing environment. To achieve stability for each major functional component of the organization that is analyzed by end user computing, there needs to be a uniformity of feedback to the business and to data processing systems, as shown in Figure 3–6.

ORGANIZATIONAL THRUST—IN SUMMARY

The information center environment, today in its infancy, is rapidly heading into an organizationally unstable state. The instability results from the high degree of autonomy of the different application-oriented end user computing groups. Although very appealing, the autonomy of the different groups leads to inconsistent results, which defeats the purpose of the information center concept.

Once the issue of inconsistency emerges, management can adopt one of three stances—do away with end user computing (which is self-defeating); take no stance and let nature take its

Functionally Similar End User Computing Groups Doing
Autonomous Processing

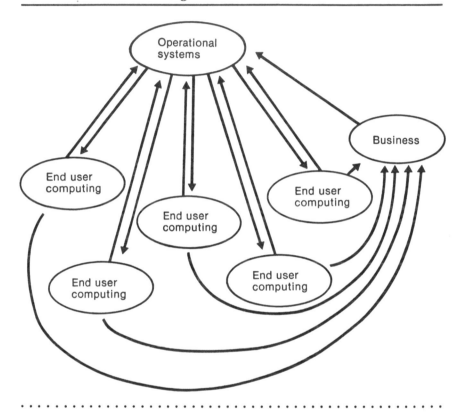

course; or insist on organizational discipline, and head for an
architected approach to end user computing. Given management's past proclivities, the best bet is that management will allow nature to take its course and let a single application-
oriented end user computing group emerge as the definitive
source for end user computing.

Once the unarchitected, undisciplined autonomy of the different end user computing groups is discarded, then the end
user computing environment is in a position to be unified and
to head for new levels of effectiveness.

The Stable End User Computing Voice

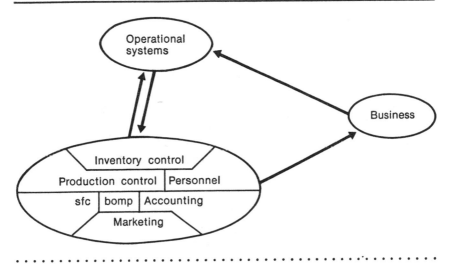

The Organizational Units

The dynamic changes in the very nature of computer usage have profound implications across all the organization. If there is ever to be an effective utilization of end user computing in the organization, there must a certain amount of discipline, and with that discipline comes an organizational infrastructure whose mandate is the architected, controlled use of data.

The traditional disciplinarian (or caretaker, in some cases) of data within the organization has been that of the data administrator (DA). In most organizations there first appeared the data base administration function that was charged with the technical maintenance and design of data base. It soon became clear that trying to address some of the basic problems of data when a project was well into physical data base design was inadequate for the recognition and control of the commonality of data across diverse application areas. Thus was born the data administration function.

Classical Data Administration

The classical DA function was usually placed within the data processing department. Typical responsibilities included building and maintenance of the data dictionary, establishment of naming standards, and so forth. In most shops the data administration's function was technoclerical. In the classical case, the DA had little influence over application development and design decisions. The typical organizational positioning of the DA is as shown in Figure 3–7. This positioning was moderately effective as long as all processing was done by data processing. But with the advent of end user computing, processing is done across the entire organization. Figure 3–8 illustrates the difference in processing before and after the advent of end user computing.

Some of the actual processing of data has shifted to the operating units with the advent of end user computing. But the scope of control of the DA has not. The result is that not even the smallest attempt to discipline the organization in the usage of data is being made. To begin to establish control, the DA function must be organizationally elevated, as shown in Figure 3–9.

F I G U R E   3–7

The Classical Domain of Data Administration

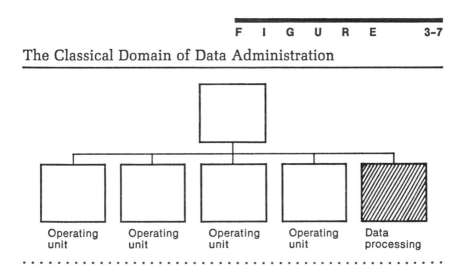

Operating unit   Operating unit   Operating unit   Operating unit   Data processing

F   I   G   U   R   E   3-8

a. Processing Data Prior to the Advent of End User Computing

b. Processing of Data after the Advent of End User Computing

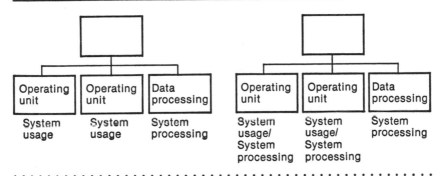

Repositioning the DA

But organizationally repositioning the DA function is only the first step in achieving organizational discipline. The DA must have a real say in certain critical design decisions. The new functions of the DA include:

Developing an architecture. The architecture includes a data model at different levels, the phases of development required for the achievement of the architecture, the analysis of how existing systems fit within that architecture, the relationship between data and process modeling at the different levels of modeling, and so forth. The architecture recognizes and accounts for commonality of processing and data, and at the same time allows differences to be handled. The DA's role includes initial construction of the architecture and periodic maintenance. The DA is not only responsible for the development of the architecture, but for the concordance of upper management—both DP and end user upper management. When there are conflicts with the architecture, it is up to the DA to bring these conflicts to management's attention and to determine the proper resolution.

To be effective in the end user computing environment, the DA must be organizationally elevated.

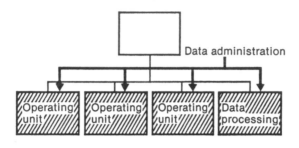

Continuing project development direction and control. The DA must be involved early on in all project development. The nature of the involvement is both advisory and controlling. The DA should have the right to review and/or make all major architectural decisions. Note that this greatly alters the status of the classical DA, who served a technoclerical function. DA involvement in the early stages of project development centers around the architecture of the shop and the conformance of any project to that architecture.

Monitoring end user computing. End user computing does not follow the same life-cycle development as does traditional DP development and does not achieve the same result. However, end user computing has its own architecture—principally a data architecture—that must be followed. It is the duty of the DA to see that end user computing is architecturally sound, much like the DA ensures that traditional DP development conforms to an architecture. Note that this span of control *greatly* differs from that of the classical DA. The end user is now subject to a completely alien organizational unit. Further complicating the role of the DA and the end user is that as the DA directs the end user in accordance with the end user architecture, it is entirely likely that the DA will have to cross organizational boundaries in addressing the issues of usage and data processing. Crossing traditional organizational lines is *sure* to increase the end user's resistance to DA control.

Aligning and executing shop's architecture in accordance with long-term strategic direction. One of the great advantages to an architecture is that at the moment of initial construction, the architecture can be directed in one of many directions. It is the job of the DA to ensure that the architecture for a shop is aligned with the long-term strategic direction of upper management and that the execution of the architecture continues the alignment.

Periodic communication and feedback to management. Given the built-in resistance of the organization to the emancipated role of the DA, the DA of necessity must be in a high-visibility role with direct access to high management when needed.

The discipline required to achieve effective end user computing then requires major organization shifts in control and attitudes. Typically organizations adapt much more readily to technical change than to organizational change. It is incumbent upon upper management to recognize the stakes involved and to ensure that the correct organizational posture is taken. Interestingly, the changes called for correspond directly to the maturing of the organization.

THE SHIFTING BUDGET FOR INFORMATION CENTER/END USER COMPUTING EXPENDITURES

Organizational restructuring is only one critical factor in the successful implementation of effective end user computing. Another major issue is budgetary responsibility. The traditional budgetary role of the data processing department has been that of purchasing or acquiring all the computer needs of the company—including hardware, software, consulting, and other goods and services. But with the advent of the information center and end user computing, there is an apparent shift in budgetary responsibility from the DP department to the end user. Consequences of the shift will profoundly shape the technoeconomic landscape of the next decade.

The Budgetary Shift

There is little doubt that *some* shift in spending habits is occurring—the only question is the extent of the shift. Some surveys

indicate that data processing is in control of the hardware/
software budget, as always. Other surveys indicate that such is
not the case. Indeed, in an interview with an IBM marketing representative, it was stated that about 80 percent of the IBM PCs
sold were directly sold to the end user. Another indication of
the shift in budgetary control is the overall spending habits as
shown by Figure 3–10. The figure shows an increasing amount
of the spending on hardware and software has been done outside of the DP department in recent years. This amount certainly
includes direct end user purchases, as well as other sources.

F   I   G   U   R   E   3-10

Data Processing Spending—Hardware, Software, Data
Communications, Data Entry, Supplies, Services

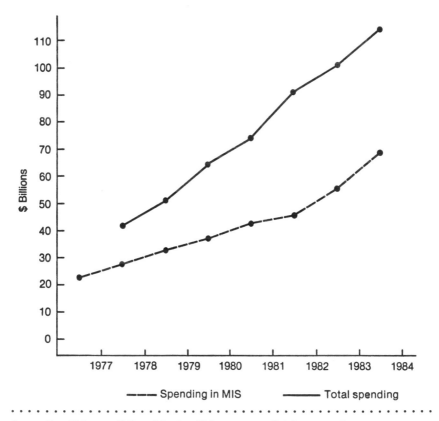

There is one plausible explanation for the controversy as to who is controlling the spending on end user products: In some cases DP establishes standards (equipment lines, software products, and so on) for end user computing, and the end user then chooses among the standards. In this case DP may claim that it is controlling expenditures because it is channeling the expenditures to a predetermined set of vendors and products. But it is the end user who determines when the purchase is made, the terms of the purchase, the specific choice of equipment, and so forth. The end user is paying directly out of his or her budget. So there may be, in some cases, a quite simple explanation for the discrepancy in opinions as to who is paying for end user computing. A change in budgetary responsibility then, is in the wind, whatever the extent or nature of the change. What then are some of the consequences of the change?

The DP Department and the Shifting Budget

The traditional attitude of DP, with its largely centralized approach to computer processing, is changing. Once the DP department was the controller of *all* processing. The emerging role for DP will be the caretaker of the operational systems of a corporation. Once data (and its attendant processing) no longer is in the operational mode, the end user assumes control. Thus the information organization of the future will be split according to the type of work occurring, based on the appropriate mode of operation.

In past years data processing established chargeback systems to try to raise the end user's awareness of the resources spent on the user's behalf. Such systems were seldom taken very seriously by end users. One direct consequence of the budgetary shift from DP to the end user is that tomorrow's chargeback systems will be only for operational processing. The end user will not need a chargeback system for expenditures, but these expenditures will come directly out of the end user's pocket.

Once paying directly for computing, the end user equates expenses for hardware and software to other direct expenditures, such as furniture and staffing. With this new-found awareness of expenditures comes a whole new attitude toward computerization. No longer is the end user spending "public money." No longer does the end user not connect system requirements with the company's bottom line.

The End User and the Budgetary Shift

The essence of end user computing is the autonomy of processing that is possible with 4GL technology and the shifting of control directly into the hands of the end user. These changes are very appealing, but inevitably an organization is faced with many small end user groups off doing their processing. In an unarchitected, undisciplined end user computing environment there is very little coordinated activity. Each end user has his or her own budget. The budget for a corporation, in total, may be quite sizable, but the budget is made up of a collection of many, small autonomous units. The result is that end user computing tends to be very decentralized, since any given user does not have the budgetary resources to even consider centralized processing. Given the magnitude of costs of the microprocessor environment, the end user who directly controls his or her own budget can be expected to gravitate to the microprocessor environment.

A by-product of the high degree of decentralization of end user computing is that end user systems will become even more DSS oriented. In a highly decentralized environment, it becomes increasingly difficult to construct operational systems. The net effect is that even if end user computing did not start off to be purely DSS, it will quickly move in that direction when the end user assumes budgetary responsibility.

A further exercise of the past—cost justification of systems—is profoundly changed. Once DP and end user engaged in the ritual of cost-justifying systems for which DP was totally responsible. Such exercises were seldom done accurately or objectively (if indeed they were done at all). After assuming budget control, end users only have to cost justify expenditures to their departments. Cost justification must occur, but now it occurs in the classical manner of all direct expenditures.

Not Shifting Control

Are all organizations allowing the budgetary shift to end user computing to occur? The answer is no. Some corporations still insist on attempting to manage end user computing expenditures as if end user computing were merely an extension of the systems built in the 1960s and 1970s.

There are too few cases to warrant making generalized statements, but several phenomena have been observed where the DP department insists on "controlling" end user computer expenses. Some of these phenomena are:

End user runs processing on a mainframe rather than the micro.

Literally thousands of users have identification that enables them to do mainframe processing.

Hardware budget for end user computing is *easily* the fastest growing portion of the entire DP expenditures.

Cost justification for end user computing is taken nonchalantly by the user as all charge back systems have been taken.

End user often attempts to build operational systems (or replacements for existing operational systems) using 4GL tools on the mainframe.

The net result is a huge morass of end user systems, the vast majority of which are unintegrated, which produce questionable results, but which undoubtedly cost much money.

The Budgetary Shift—Summary

The advent of end user computing has given birth to a shift in the spending habits of corporations on hardware and software. This shift has fundamentally changed the corporate attitude toward buying. With the change in attitude came a shift in the types of equipment being bought, the uses of that equipment, and the purpose of the equipment. In addition, the entire approach to cost justification has changed radically as well—from an approach of spending "other people's money," to the direct expenditure of departmental money.

THE INFORMATION ORGANIZATION

The traditional organization chart and the traditional data processing organization of the 1960s to the present is inadequate to handle the information needs of today. The inadequacies of the organization range from the inability to account for end user computing to the inability of the DP organization to relate to the direct business of the serviced company. In short, the traditional DP organization is an anachronism that once served a viable purpose but has been passed up by time and circumstance. Replacing (or superimposing itself) over the traditional DP organization is what can be termed the "information organization." The information organization must be able to account for an organization's overall needs for data and information over all modes of operation. What then are modes of operation?

Modes of Operation

The two major (but certainly not only) modes of operation accommodated by the information organization are the operational and the end user computing (or DSS) modes of operation.

Each of these modes of operation has its own separate, yet related, architecture. The construction of and usage of the operational architecture is discussed at length in W. H. Inmon's *Information Systems Architecture* (Prentice-Hall, 1986) and *Integrating Data Processing Systems: In Theory and in Practice* (Prentice-Hall, 1984). The purpose of the operational architecture is to:

Identify *all* major system operational requirements.

Identify commonality of data and processing across all requirements.

Recognize differences across all requirements.

Fit common and unique data and processing requirements into a single framework.

Given the tools of the operational environment, it is necessary to rigidly define requirements at a complete and low level of detail. The difficulty of change in and of itself necessitates the need for complete and detailed definitions of requirements. The resulting architecture for operational systems reflects the need to define operational systems at a low level of detail. But the architecture for end user computing is much more flexible, primarily due to the tools that are available in the end user computing environment, the nature of the environment, and the emphasis on data, not processes, in that environment.

The end user computing architecture focuses on data, and data at a high level of abstraction, with details organized accordingly. The information organization then supports two architectures—an operational (or data processing) architecture, and an end user computing architecture. (Note: The description of how to build an end user computing architecture and a detailed example of the architecture is described in Chapter 6 of this book.)

These architectures are held together by the high-level corporate data model—commonly known as the corporate ERD— or corporate entity-relationship diagram. The high level ERD for the operational architecture is the *same* ERD for the end user computing architecture. If there are differences between them there will predictably be *major* problems with the corporate information organizations.

Architectural Relationships

The relationship of the two architectures is shown by Figure 3–11. Although the relationship between the two architectures is straightforward at the ERD level, or highest level of data modeling, what is not clear is that the corporate model is constantly changing. The ERD model, with its attendant operational and end user computing architectures, is a dynamic model, constantly changing. But because the ERD has been constructed to reflect all business needs at the most abstract level, the changes to the ERD (and consequently to the related architectures) are at a low level of detail, normally not affecting the ERD. Only in the case of major business changes, where the ERD is drastically altered, are the changes felt at the high level of modeling.

There are some architectural differences between the operational and end user computing architectures that are worth noting at this point. The operational architecture normally extends down to a low level of detail, since operational processing must be rigidly defined. But the end user computing architecture extends only to the high level model of the ERD, since end user computing first depends on data, then secondarily on processing. The needs of end user computing are dynamic and fluid, and it is improper to rigidly define its architecture, as is the operational architecture. The implication is that the world of end user computing is so flexible and views data so many different ways that it does not make sense to model end user computing requirements to a low level of detail. Instead end user computing requirements are only unified at the highest level of modeling, the ERD level.

F I G U R E   3–11

Relationship of the Operational and End User Computing Architectures

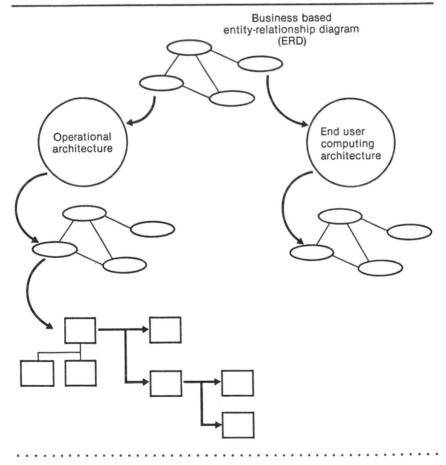

THE ARCHITECTURES AND THE ORGANIZATION CHART

The relationship of the end user computing architecture, the operational architecture, and the business of the company are directly related to the organization chart, as shown by Figure 3–12. The figure shows that top management relates to business and direction of the organization, that DP is the caretaker for the operational systems of the company, and that the separate operating units are the owners and caretakers of end user computing. To ensure adherence to the architectures, the DA serves as the organizational unit monitoring the administration of architectural compliance across the organization. Once again the role and the scope of the DA function are stressed.

Another perspective is that information processing has traditionally been divided up into the functions of strategic, tacti-

F I G U R E   3-12

Organization Chart Geared to Meet the Needs of
Organizational Functions

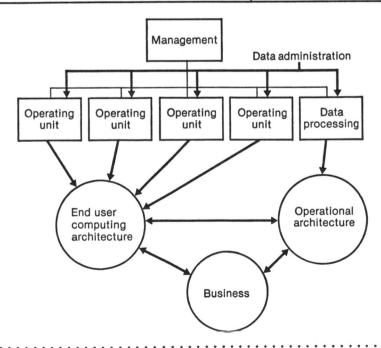

cal, and operational processing, as shown by Figure 3–13. Unfortunately the figure gives the impression that the information organization is neatly divided into different categories of data. Such is an oversimplification, which at best clouds the real issue of the information organization. A more realistic representation of the information organization is shown by Figure 3–14.

TOP MANAGEMENT AND THE INFORMATION ORGANIZATION

A major component of the effectiveness of the information organization is how responsive the organization is to top management. The very foundations of the information organization— the end user computing architecture and the data processing architecture—lend themselves to communication with top management, since the basis for those architectures is the ERD, and the ERD addresses the business of the organization at the highest level of abstraction. Top management generally thinks in global terms, so it is natural for management to refer to the organization in the same abstract terms found in the ERD. The result is that an architected end user computing environment and data processing environment fit very nicely into top management plans.

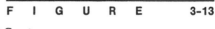

F   I   G   U   R   E   3-13

A Traditional Classification of Systems

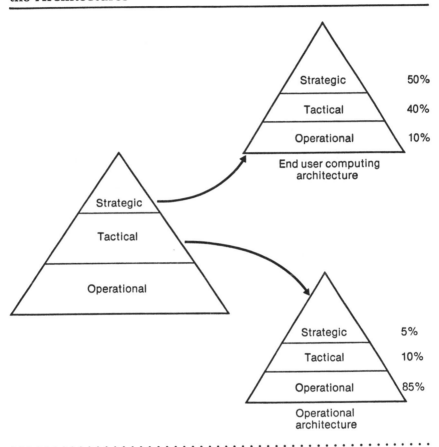

Strategic, Tactical, and Operational Implications of the Architectures

Organizational Dynamics of the Information Organization

The information organization can be viewed abstractly as management interacting with two architectures through the DA. Although this view is correct, it nevertheless is so abstract that the dynamics of the interactions are hard to see. A simple example will illustrate the dynamics of the end user computing architecture, the data processing architecture, and management.

Figure 3–15 illustrates a bank operations. A customer goes to a teller to transact bank business. The teller uses DP systems

The Information Cycle

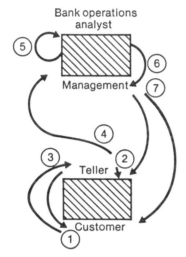

1. Customer submits detailed request to teller.
2. Teller uses DP system in the servicing of request.
3. Reply to customer comes from teller or DP system
4. Massive amounts of detailed transaction data are sent to EUC analyst for analysis.
5. Iterated analysis by the EUC analyst occurs.
6. The analyst delivers results and recommendations to management.
7. Management makes decisions that affect the entire class of customers either indirectly or through DP systems.

to determine what action to take. Then either the teller or the DP system itself affects the action. The details of all transactions are stored and are periodically passed to end user computing. Once the analyst has the detailed data to work with, an iterated set of analyses is affected.

The analyst heuristically manipulates the data until a set of recommendations is prepared for management. Once management receives the recommendations, decisions are made to act or not act on them. Once management decides to act, the result is an indirect effect on the class of customers as a whole (such as the lowering of interest rates) or the actual altering of the data processing system itself.

End User Computing and Cost Justification

The feedback loop of Figure 3-15 can be used to make some interesting observations about the cost justification of end user computing, which can be measured according to two criteria—effectiveness and efficiency. End user computing systems usually lend themselves to effectiveness more than efficiency.

The payback of the effectiveness must be measured at a gross level, since direct measurement is almost impossible. Instead, the payback of end user computing should be done on an environmental basis (i.e., is the end user computing environment—not a single end user system—proving to be worthwhile?).

Auditing the File

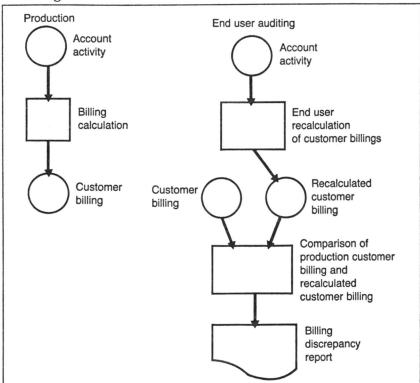

The end user has taken the customer activity data and has independently audited the file, recalculating the amount billed. Then the recalculated amount is compared with the billed amount to determine discrepancies. The worth of the end user computing system can be stated as the difference between the summarized billed amount and the summarized recalculated billed amount. Of course the difference may be negative, at which point the value of billing the customer the correct amount must be calculated.

The feedback loop of Figure 3–15 suggests that a measurement can be done, but the measurement comes indirectly in the measurement of very gross indicators of prosperity, such as gross revenue, gross profit, and market share. One approach is to map the spending, activity, and so on of end user computing against one or more meaningful indications of prosperity, as suggested by Figure 3–16.

An obvious and major problem with the correlation suggested in Figure 3–16 is that the prosperity indicator may actually have nothing (either positively or negatively) to do with end user computing. Other external business factors *must* be accounted for in reviewing the correlation. In short, end user computing does not supplant good judgment and common sense—it only serves to broaden the basis for better judgment and better common sense. Furthermore, to be effective, the results of end user computing *must* reach top management, where the major decision and directions are taken. The effectiveness can best be optimized by placing end user computing in the most critical parts of the company. Not much is needed to be effective, only end user computing that is well positioned. In this regard end user computing may not be entirely appropriate for middle-level or low-level management. In the final analysis

F   I   G   U   R   E   3–16

Correlating the Activity of End User Computing with a Businesswide Prosperity Indicator

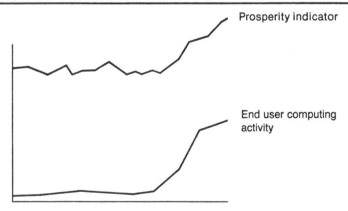

then, the best measurements of the effectiveness of end user computing are:

Does top management feel satisfied that it has a better grip on the activities of the company as a result of end user computing?

How does the prosperity of the business correlate to the activities of end user computing?

Is the end user computing that is occurring being directed at the central, most critical parts of the business?

In short, to be effective, end user computing must address top management and must address the most critical aspects of the business. An invitation for waste occurs when end user computing is directed at middle to lower management and when it is aimed at noncritical business functions.

End User Efficiency

The efficiency of end user computing can be calculated a bit more analytically than can effectiveness:

End user computing advantage = Development Δ
     + Operating Δ

When the end user computing advantage goes less than zero, it is advantageous to build the system with traditional tools; when it is greater than zero, then it is advantageous to build the system with end user computing tools. A further explanation of the above formula follows.

End user computing advantage = Development Δ + Operating
     development Δ = Traditional development costs − End
     user computing development costs
Operating Δ = (Traditional unit operating costs × Number
     of executions) − (End user unit operating costs × Number
     of executions)

These formulas are best brought to light in terms of some examples. Suppose:

> End user development costs = $100
> Traditional development costs = $10,000
> End user unit operating costs = $125

Traditional unit operating costs = $25
Expected number of times executed = 20

Then:

$$Development = 10,000 - 100 = 9,900$$
$$Operating\ cost = (25 \times 20) - (125 \times 20)$$
$$= 500 - 2,500 = -2,000$$
$$End\ user\ computing\ advantage = 9,900 + (-2,000) = 7,900$$

In this case it is efficient to build the system with end user computing tools, but suppose the number of expected executions rose to 10,000. Then:

$$Development = 10,000 - 100 = 9,900$$
$$Operating\ cost = (25 \times 10,000) - (125 \times 10,000)$$
$$= 250,000 - 1,250,000 = -1,000,000$$
$$End\ user\ computing\ advantage = 9,900 + (-1,000,000)$$
$$= -990,100$$

The advantage is clearly in the negative, so it is advantageous to build the system with traditional development tools. Notice that the formulas are simplified for the purpose of discussions. In reality they can be greatly enhanced to account for many more subtleties. However, the basic factors do not change, nor do the conclusions derived from the analysis.

The efficiency is an entirely different issue than effectiveness in end user computing. Efficiency is easy to measure, and effectiveness is hard to measure; and usage of end user computing for efficiency is widespread, but usage of end user computing for effectiveness is rather limited. The issues of effectiveness and efficiency can be related to the basic relationship chart as described in Figure 1–7. The issues of efficiency relate to the direct DP/end user relationship, and the issues of effectiveness relate to the indirect relationship, as shown by Figure 3–17.

SUMMARY

The information center is the organizational unit by which most end user computing organizations initially approach computing. But the classical autonomy of end user processing leads

F   I   G   U   R   E   3–17

Effectiveness and Efficiency in End User Computing and
Data Processing

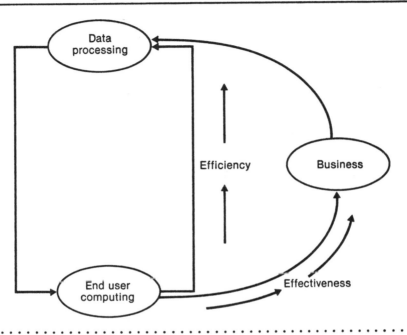

to an unstable environment. Predictably, end user computing
departments that overlap in function do not produce consistent
results. The evolution there is toward an architected, stabi-
lized end user computing organization, where there is uniformity of results. Part of the realization of the architecture is the
organizational change of the data administration function.
From a technoclerical background, data administration is elevated to a portion of real design and development responsibility
and authority. The DA is changed with the creation of an architecture, the ongoing maintenance of the architecture, and the
conformance to the architecture of the various end user computing groups. Budget responsibility is a major part of the
organizational shift in attitudes and practices. The end user
must assure direct budgetary responsibility for the resources
consumed.

Finally, the worth of end user computing can be measured by the effectiveness and efficiency of end user computing. Effectiveness is measured indirectly, according to major prosperity indicators. Efficiency can be measured by the trade-off in development and operation costs between operational and end user computing systems.

DIRECTIVES AND DIRECTIONS

- End user computing has many organizational implications—to the traditional data processing department, to the end user, to management, and so forth.
- The first manifestation of end user computing usually comes in the form of an information center.
- The information center usually springs spontaneously.
- The information center is usually oriented toward different end user applications.
- The orientation toward different applications leads to a lack of credibility, since each application has (not surprisingly!) its own autonomous processing.
- The stable end user computing environment is oriented around a standard operating environment and an application-independent data architecture. The intent of the data architecture is to allow major differences of opinion between end user analysts to be resolved.
- The classical role of the data administrator is improperly placed to effectively administrate the end user computing architecture. To be effective, the data administrator must be greatly elevated organizationally.
- The mature end user computing environment pays directly for its own expenditures for hardware and software. Chargeback systems or no budgetary feedback are unacceptable for the mature organization.
- One reason for the need for direct budgetary responsibility is the huge amount of resources consumed by the tools of end user computing.
- End user computing and traditional data processing are so different that they form two modes of operation linked

together by a data model, which is at the heart of the data architecture.

- One way of approaching the cost justification of end user computing is to compare the trade-off between development and operating costs.
- Another way of approaching the cost justification is to determine the payback of end user computing on a system-by-system basis.

Establishing the End User
Computing Environment

• •

The traditional data processing organization usually serves as the focal point for establishing the end user computing environment. One is bombarded with ads from the media proclaiming the advantages of end user computing, but when actually building the environment, the end user usually relies on the corporate DP department for advice on selection, installation, and usage of the hardware and software.

In this role the DP department serves to unify (at least architecturally) the hardware and software through such institutions as the standard operating environment. In those instances where there is no architecturally unifying organization, there is only a small chance that there will be any consistency of hardware and software across the computing environment.

The nature of end user computing is one of autonomous processing—wherein one is free to process data unfettered by external controls. There is therefore seldom any force compelling one to commit to doing end user computing, but one is lured or enticed into it. The most effective entry into the end user computing environment is for the interested party to *sell* the end user.

THE ORIGINS

Contrast the advent of end user computing with the advent of data processing. The original motivation for data processing was for more efficiency through the automation of normal business practices. Top management was sold on the inherent efficiencies of data processing and the economies of scale that were possible, and soon computers and programmers arrived. The marketing and selling of computers that was done was at a high corporate level. Once sold, the corporation commenced to automate. But end user computing has for the most part, been sold at a much lower corporate level, and very few coordinated end user computing implementations have been made. Instead, end user computing has grown up spontaneously and at an uneven pace throughout the organization.

The following represents some typical tools and techniques by which DP plays a role of leadership in establishing the end user computing environment.

Newsletter. Establish a newsletter to describe end user computing successes, problems, breakthroughs, and so forth. Make sure names and positions are included so that an informal network can be fostered. Publish the newsletter frequently enough so that readers rely on the newsletter to keep up with innovations.

Open house. Periodically hold open houses, featuring demonstrations of equipment, software, applications, and the like. Make sure other users are on hand to share experiences. Use open houses to expand end user computing visibility across the organization and up and down the organization.

Demonstrations. Schedule personalized demonstrations of equipment and software. Make sure the presentation addresses the particular needs of the audience for whom the demonstration is made. Use demonstrations to build the end user computing network.

Online tutorial. Create or acquire an online tutorial so that the end user, immediately upon acquiring equipment and software, can use the tutorial in a "self-help" mode. In addition to freeing the DP liaison and training staff, this approach has the effect of quickly conditioning the end user to an atmosphere of autonomy.

Seminars. Conduct seminars on subjects of interest to the end user community. Include both experienced end users and neophytes in the seminars. Use both in-house and external sources in the delivery of the seminar. Vary the seminar subject material over time to appeal to a wide audience. Present the seminars frequently enough to create an air of continuity and dependency.

Free trial. Arrange for the end user to use equipment on a free trial basis. Depending on the budgetary arrangements, the free trial may be paid for by DP or by the vendor.

Classes. Conduct regular classes that cover the basic use and care of end user equipment and software. Hold classes at both a basic and an advanced level.

ONCE THE ENVIRONMENT IS ESTABLISHED

Once the end user computing environment is established, the overseer and sponsoring function of DP continues. Some of the functions of the ongoing challenge of coordinating the end user computing environment may include:

Vendor relations. DP coordinates purchases, exchanges, monitors problems, and so forth. Usually a fair discount can be obtained by group purchase of equipment, rather than a series of individual purchases. In addition, a single conduit from a vendor to the entire body of end users is useful for such things as new product announcements and product enhancements.

Critical point for troubleshooting. When a user has a problem or simply gets stuck, it is useful to have a central referral point. The DP liaison function naturally fills this role. Hotline service or individual attention tends to reinforce the support of the DP department. In the eventuality that the vendor must be contacted, it is more efficient to have a single clearing point that is geared for regular vendor contact than it is to have each end user establish that contact.

Resource utilization monitoring. Some end user resources will be stressed; others will be underused. It is useful for resource utilization to be monitored so that resources can be balanced according to need.

THE END USER LEARNING CURVES

There are (at least!) two learning curves through which the end user must traverse—the learning curve of how to use end user equipment and software, and the learning curve of how to apply the newly learned technology to the end user's environment. Both learning curves are essential to the success of the end user computing environment.

The first learning curve—how to use the equipment and software—is fairly straightforward. Included in this curve are such topics as:

What equipment the end user is to use.

What software is to be used.

How to "log on" and "log off."

How to access data.

Seminar Topics of Interest to End Users

> New features of spreadsheet software.
>
> Getting data to/from the mainframe.
>
> Storing and reusing trend-analysis data.
>
> Passing results to another end user.
>
> Securing your data and your PC.
>
> Adding memory to your PC—how to do it—what it will do for you.
>
> Case studies—successes and failures.
>
> Panel discussions—reconciling conflicting reports.
>
> Beyond spreadsheets—effective use of other end user tools.
>
> How other companies are using end user tools.
>
> Seminars and meetings that are used to promote end user computing should be imaginative and designed to stimulate the users. Over time, a wide variety of people should be allowed and encouraged to attend and participate in the seminars.

How to manipulate data.

How to produce reports.

How to pass data to other users, and so forth.

The basics the end user must master are fairly obvious. The second learning curve—how to apply the end user computing tools to the end user's environment—is not nearly so obvious. The second learning curve includes:

What specific data is available to the end user.

What the costs of end user computing are.

What the end user does with the results, once analysis is complete.

How the usage of the computer can make the end user's job either more efficient or more effective.

What limitations the end user needs to be aware of.

In short, the second learning curve (which is perhaps more important than the first) must be tailored individually to each user. Unfortunately, there exists little (and it is unlikely there will ever exist much) training material for the second learning curve, since each application of end user computing is so individualized.

The End User's Exposure to the Architecture

Creating the effective end user computing environment requires establishment of and adherence to an end user computing architecture. After end users have been initiated into the basic environment, another level of training—exposure to the architecture—ensues. They must first be informed that there is an architecture. Next a long discussion describes why an architecture is necessary. Part of this discussion necessarily addresses the difficulty of achieving effectiveness without an architecture. Following this discussion the actual architecture is described. Along with the overall view of the architecture, end users are pointed to further sources for more detailed information. Next they are told how the architecture helps build sys-

Data for Periodic Trend Analysis

Base data for periodic trend analysis:

Monthly account balance.

Monthly number of deposits.

Monthly average deposit amount.

Monthly number, amount overdrafts.

Monthly linked account processes.

Monthly number, amount withdrawals.

Monthly average amount of withdrawals.

Using the above data, which is stored each month, the bank produces two trend analysis reports—summarized account balance by month and summarized average account balance by month. The trends are plotted by month. Using the stored base data, many other reports can be generated; but because of the granularity and content of data, there are many other types of analyses that cannot be generated—

Weekly trends.

Daily trends.

Minimum balance analysis.

Maximum balance analysis.

Geographic analysis, trends.

The content and granularity of data that is used as a basis for trend analysis greatly influences the ways the data can be used. The finer the granularity and the more measurement and storage of data, the more future flexibility the analyst will have.

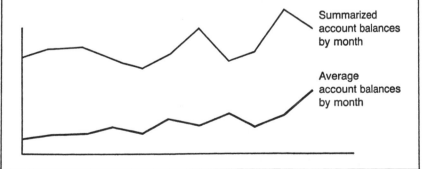

tems quickly. The advantages and uses of the architecture are stressed, as well as what positive benefits there are to an architecture. In addition, users are introduced to the data administration representative responsible to their general application area. The final perspective is what is expected of end users in terms of conformance to the architecture. This discussion is held with an emphasis on the positive. In short, the final formal education all end users receive as part of their indoctrination addresses the architecture.

SUMMARY

Part of the initiation process is selling the concept to the end user. This is accomplished through such vehicles as:

Newsletters.

Open houses.

Demonstrations.

Online tutorials.

Seminars.

Free trials.

Classes.

Once the end user is sold, a certain amount of standard training is required.

To establish the end user computing environment requires at least three levels of education and indoctrination.

Introduction to hardware and software.

How end user tools apply to the job.

Introduction to the end user computing architecture.

DIRECTIVES AND DIRECTIONS

- The end user computing environment grows best in an atmosphere in which end user computing is fostered.

Some fostering techniques for the initial impetus of end user computing include:

Newsletters.

Open houses.

Demonstrations.

Online tutorials.

Seminars.

Classes.

- Despite the dispersed nature of end user computing, there is a need for a focal point that serves to centralize vendor relations, troubleshooting, and so on.
- The end user goes through two learning curves—an initial learning curve as to how to use the technology and a secondary learning curve as to how to apply the technology to the end user's everyday job.
- A final aspect of the "conditioning" of the end user is introduction to the concept of an architecture. The introduction discusses the need for an architecture, what is required to conform to the architecture, and the roles of the data administrator and chief information officer.

Using End User Computing Technology

●●●●●●●●●●●●●●●●●●●●●●●●●●●●●●●●●●

If any mode of operation can be depicted as having diverse usages, it is end user computing. The span of activities encom-
passed by end user computing ranges from financial modeling
to prototyping to trend analysis and monitoring. Typical end
users range from financial analysts to managers to manufacturing quality control personnel. This diversity in users and usages
of end user computing has sprung up even in the face of the
short time (relative to other forms of computing) that end user
computing has existed.

There are different criteria for success, different issues, and
different characteristics for the various kinds of end user computing. This chapter will explore some of the more common
forms of end user computing and will address their salient
points.

TREND ANALYSIS

Trend analysis occurs for regularly measured events, such as
quarterly profits, monthly production, weekly price fluctu-
ations, or annual measurement of number of employees. This
tool is used by management to determine relative progress (or
lack thereof) toward some goal.

Whatever trend is being measured is scaled against some
appropriate time differential, and the measurement usually oc-

curs as a summary or average of meaningful indicators. Usually a breakout of numbers that constitute the final measurement is available. For example, if corporate profitability is being measured quarterly, then the contributions to profit by sales divisions, by line of business, by geographic region, and so forth are usually available.

Trend analysis may fall under the category of regularly scheduled reporting, in which case, it is not—strictly speaking—a function of end user computing. But when management wants a detailed, complex, customized analysis done above and beyond the regular trend report (usually to explain the regularly scheduled report!) end user computing often enters.

Some of the issues of end user computing for trend analysis are:

Inability to vary time parameters for historic data. Once trends begin to be measured, the unit of time over which they are measured is set, and it is very difficult, if not impossible, to vary that unit of time after the fact. For example, suppose a trend analysis is done quarterly, and management wishes to reanalyze the trend monthly. This can be done only if the base data has been kept in a very detailed format.

Inability to vary other parameters of measurement. Once the regularly scheduled analysis is produced, it may or may not be easy to revisit the data and produce a related but different analysis. For example, if simple employment of a company is being measured annually, there is analysis about the growth of the pany. But simple annual employment says nothing about employment turnover (i.e., how many hired, how many left the company), even though the figures are closely related.

Inability to extrapolate data. When measuring data over time, extrapolation can prove to be dangerous or at least misleading. As a simple example, on Monday Bill Biddle has $50 in his savings account, on Tuesday Bill deposits $1,000. On Thursday Bill withdraws $950, and on Friday his account has $100 in it. If Bill's account is measured on Monday and Friday (i.e., at $50 and at $100), his account will show that on Tuesday he had $62.50, on Wednesday he had $75.00, and on Thursday he had

$87.50. This of course is not reflective at all of his real account balance, but points out the danger in measuring data at discrete moments and drawing conclusions about the moments not measured (which is a common practice in trend analysis).

Interpretation of trends. It is one thing to measure trends and another the interpret them. If the profitability of a company turns upward, the upturn can be measured. But there is *always* speculation as to the cause. Perhaps management is good; perhaps the marketplace conditions are such that *any* company in the marketplace would show growth and profitability; perhaps the sale of capital equipment influences the profit picture, and so forth. In this regard—ferreting out the reasons behind the large picture—end user computing can be a real asset.

Because the selection algorithms for the base data on which the trend analysis is run are usually set once (at the outset), it makes sense to select data (and store the data) at the most granular level feasible. This means storing data with very small time increments and at a detailed level. By doing so, the trend analysis can be revisited at a later time so that later analysis is not limited to the variables and units of time of the primary trend analysis. For example, suppose corporate profitability is to be measured quarterly. One approach is to simply store the profits or losses of the corporation by quarter. However, at a later time, it will be very difficult to revisit the analysis based on other criteria—such as, by line of business, what have the profitability trends been? or what have the divisional profits been by month? To revisit the corporate profit trend at a later time requires storing of the summarized data concerning corporate profitability. In this case, storing by month data concerning corporate profitability by line of business and by division of the company allows the analysis to be revisited at a later time.

Such storage of data that feeds a trend analysis system is an *appendage* of data, as opposed to a true update of data. Each month (or whatever the appropriate unit of time), the monthly results are simply appended onto the accumulation of previous months' data. The process of appendage amounts to an archiving of data. One issue that *always* arises with the archival of data is how much data to keep. Over time, the amount of data stored adds up.

Trend analysis and exception reporting is usually done at a technoclerical level, sometimes directly by the end user and sometimes by technicians acting on behalf of the end user.

The worth of trend analysis is fairly obvious. When important trends are identified early (or in some cases, identified at all) the corporation is in a position to respond. To be effective then, the analytical activities need to be able to be communicated at the appropriate level of management, which generally is high within the organization. One of the pitfalls of trend analysis is that it is inherently a reactive activity. That is, the company is in a position to react as opposed to anticipate, as in other proactive end user computing activities. The worth of trend analysis is measured by its effectiveness, not its efficiency. Therefore, as with other effectiveness-oriented end user computing, trend analysis should be aimed at the mainstream of the corporation and at a high level of management.

AD HOC REPORTING

An ad hoc report is one that is issued on a one-time or nonrecurring basis. Ad hoc reports are found everywhere—in banking, insurance, government, manufacturing environments—to name a few. If there is a generic end user computing product, it is ad hoc reporting. It is typically produced in response to a need for in-depth exploration of some phenomena, such as why this month's expenses were so high or why this quarter's profits varied significantly from those of previous months. Ad hoc reporting involves selecting, summation, sorting, and other manipulation of data that is done on a full-form selective basis.

The tools of end user computing are uniquely equipped to do ad hoc reporting. The flexibility, the power of the language, and the very intent of end user computing tools naturally lend themselves to ad hoc reporting. Indeed, the very ease with which reports can be created and changed leads to the question, Why aren't all reports generated with end user computing tools?

The basic comparison of traditional development and operational costs versus end user computing developing and operational costs determines whether or not it is cost effective to build a report using end user computing tools. Certainly for a

Feeding End User Data

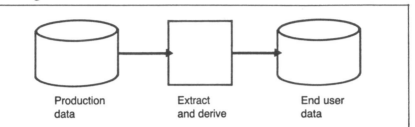

| Production
data | Extract
and derive | End user
data |

The normal way that end user data is fed from production data is by means of an extract program that accesses the dynamic production data and selects certain records for processing in the end user environment. The extraction and derivation of production data has the effect of "freezing" the data as of the moment the extract was made. However, given the nature of end user computing, the freezing of data has very little if any impact on the validity of end user processing. Given the nature of end user/decision support processing, the up-to-the-second accuracy of production data is simply unnecessary.

- What is the average balance?
- What is the average balance of customers with an account older than five years?
- What is the average balance, average number of monthly deposits of customers with accounts older than five years?
- What is the average balance, average number of monthly deposits, average size of deposit for customers with ZIP code 80303?

report that is only run once or twice, the productivity possible with end user computing tools mandates their use. It is when a report is run repeatedly, and especially when the report manipulates much data, that it becomes cost effective to use traditional development for reporting.

The documentation for ad hoc reporting often includes nothing more than the programming listing used to produce the report. When a report is being iterated, the lack of documentation is not a problem. But when the final report is produced, it usually makes sense to document, *at the least,* the following:

Input source and any selection algorithms used.

Program logic used.

Date and time the report was run.

Any miscellaneous information, such as the environment the report was produced in, for whom the report was produced, whether or not the report will be produced again, and so forth.

Of the above documentation, two components are most important—the programming algorithms used and a description of the input. Without a description of the input and any selection algorithms, the report can never be reproduced. If there is any question as to the report's validity, the question cannot meaningfully be addressed later. The assumptions underlying the report are often lost, thereby opening to question the reliability and believability of the report.

Ironically then, documentation of the final product plays an important part in end user computing in general and in ad hoc reporting in particular.

In addition to the lack of documentation, another pitfall of the ad hoc report is that it can be used to replace operational reports. In this case the cost of end user development and operation is significantly higher than the cost of traditional development and operation. The cost imbalance can be attributed to the relatively inefficient operations of end user software.

Ad hoc reporting, like trend analysis, is done at a techno-clerical level, usually within the end user department, but possibly by a technician on the behalf of the end user. Also like trend analysis, it is a reactive activity and addresses the effectiveness of the operation, not the efficiency of the operation. The worth of ad hoc reports, like all effective end user computing, is measured indirectly by the rise and fall of major prosperity indicators.

LIVING SAMPLES

Both ad hoc reporting and trend analysis can be done on live sets of data. But the volume of data is often such that the end user computing software/hardware will not handle the data, or if it can handle the data, it cannot do so in an expeditious fashion. When the volume of data grows universally, one technique is to produce living samples (or living sample data bases).

A living sample data base is one that represents the mix of data from which it is derived, but is much less voluminous.

Typically a living sample data base may be 1/10th to 1/50th as large as the original data base.

The selection of the data that goes into the living sample is of crucial importance. Ideally, data is selected so that any profile of data taken from the living sample will be identical (or at least very close) to the profile of data that would have resulted from the original set of data. To effectively create a living sample data base requires that there be no bias in the selections of data for the living sample.

The advantages of a properly constructed living sample data base are obvious. The reduction in amount of data may allow the end user to process on a micro, or the reduction may mean that results can be achieved in 10 minutes as opposed to overnight.

Use of living samples is widespread, but they are most frequently found in financial institutions and insurance companies. One immediate advantage of a properly constructed living sample data base is that the "what if" variables often associated with ad hoc reporting or trend analysis can be inexpensively changed. After deciding upon the appropriate set of ad hoc variables, the end user can run the processing against the larger, live data base.

Living sample processing is done by companies who must make global decisions based on a large sampling of data. Design of, selection of data for, and maintenance of living sample data bases is usually done by a technical function, such as data administration. However, use of a living sample data base is almost always directly in the hands of the end user.

The issues of effectiveness and efficiency are mixed. The primary *raison d'etre* for a living sample data base is effectiveness of processing. Like other effectiveness measures of worth, the value is measured by the rise and fall of prosperity indicators; but efficiency can be calculated by measuring the number of runs made against the living sample times the cost of making those runs times the number of times the actual data base is larger than the living sample. A cost effectiveness worth can be calculated by this formula:

Living sample worth = Number of usages × Cost of single
usage ×
Number of times actual data base is
larger than living sample

Living Sample Data Base

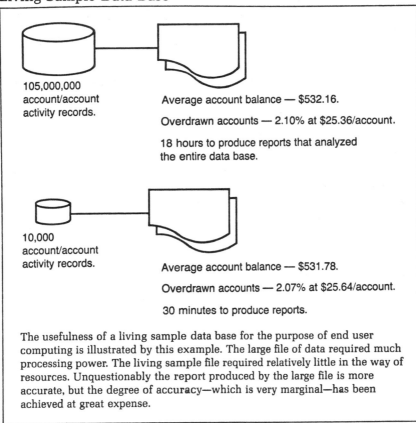

105,000,000 account/account activity records.

Average account balance — $532.16.

Overdrawn accounts — 2.10% at $25.36/account.

18 hours to produce reports that analyzed the entire data base.

10,000 account/account activity records.

Average account balance — $531.78.

Overdrawn accounts — 2.07% at $25.64/account.

30 minutes to produce reports.

The usefulness of a living sample data base for the purpose of end user computing is illustrated by this example. The large file of data required much processing power. The living sample file required relatively little in the way of resources. Unquestionably the report produced by the large file is more accurate, but the degree of accuracy—which is very marginal—has been achieved at great expense.

Demographic Analysis

A common type of living sample analysis is demographic analysis. Demographic analysis aims at analytical profiles of a population (usually, but not necessarily, a human population). Where people live, how much they spend, where they go, their living standards—all are typical uses of demographic analysis. From this analysis, marketing and manufacturing analysts formulate their strategy.

Some of the pitfalls of demographic analysis lie in the accuracy and timeliness of the base data. The analysis can be no more accurate than the selection criteria used in building the demographic analysis data base. Often the raw data comes from outside of the organization, so any bias may not be apparent. Another difficulty is in the volume of data that must be manipulated. Even creating a living sample presents its own problems in the face of an external source of much raw demographic data. There may be multiple bias of living sample external demographic data.

The worth of demographic analysis is in both its effectiveness and efficiency. In the case where the effectiveness of demographic analysis is being considered, the worth is measured in terms of the rise or fall of prosperity indicators. In the case of demographic analysis, there can be more than a general inference made when the prosperity indicator is market share. In the case of measurement of efficiency, the worth can be calculated by measuring sales made directly as a result of demographic analysis.

Demographic analysis is especially useful for companies engaged in distribution. But even for wholesalers, manufacturers, or others, understanding the marketplace is equally important, even though the direct distribution is done through other channels.

PROJECTIONS—MODELS

Another important form of end user computing is creating projections or models, such as financial models. This type of end user computing differs from other forms in that modeling normally is not fed data on which to operate, as in the case of ad hoc reporting or trend analysis. Instead, in modeling the end user is given some basic parameters (or assumptions), and the modeling commences based on the assumptions. In this light ad hoc reports or trend analysis can be classified as processing data, and modeling is more of an analytical, number manipulation activity. Interestingly, it is common for the output of trend analysis and ad hoc reporting to supply the basic parameters for modeling. In this sense modeling is fed by raw data originating from the operational environment or externally, but only after the raw data has been refined.

The salient aspects of modeling include the assumptions that set the stage for the model. By varying the assumptions, the modeler can effectively alter the outcome of the model. For this reason it is very important to document the assumptions made.

It is likewise important to document the actual model—the calculations, the flow of data, and so forth.

One pitfall of modeling is that the mistakes in the model or in the assumptions tend to proliferate themselves. A 5 percent error in year one turns into a 7.5 percent error in year two, a 10 percent error in year three, and so forth. An effective model will allow the parameters to be varied easily, will allow the intermediate calculations to be displayed, will allow the basic algorithm(s) to be inspected, and will allow the time units (year, month, quarter, day, etc.) to be varied easily.

It is normal to use a model repetitively, making minor changes until the desired analysis is achieved. Once the analysis has been done, given the customized nature of the modeling process, it is unusual to reuse the model. Modeling is used in many organizations—such as banks, insurance companies, and manufacturing firms. As useful as models are, they do not replace human control or thought. The model is only as good as the analyst creating and using it. If there are basic misunderstandings or a lack of understanding of the modeling process, the model will undoubtedly produce incorrect results. Unfortunately, the very existence of the model may produce an unwarranted level of security when the modeler has built it under incorrect assumptions. In general, documentation for the usage of modeling software is sparse. Because of the lack of documentation, learning by trial and error is the norm. As the industry matures, it is predictable that better and more documentation will be forthcoming.

There is a wide range in the length of time a typical analyst needs to create a model. A simple model can be created by an experienced analyst in a few hours. A complex model may require as much as several weeks to construct by even an experienced analyst.

Projections represent an entirely different perspective than do other forms of end user computing—a proactive use of end user computing, as opposed to a reactive use. Because projections are proactive, they rarely process much data (although they normally base their assumptions on the summarized results of reactive processing). The worth of projections is not measured in terms of the efficiency of processing. Instead worth is measured by comparing the accuracy of the projections versus actual results achieved. Unlike other measures of effectiveness, an actual value can be calculated, but by that time it is too late to act on the basis of the projection.

EXTERNAL DATA BASES

External data bases do not represent a unique form of end user computing. However, in some environments much of the effectiveness of end user computing is directly tied to the ability to access external data bases. External data bases are those that are available for processing whose source is not operational data. A typical source is commercial data bases that reflect marketing, demographic, or other raw data. External data bases are subject to the same pitfalls as other data bases—they can reflect the same bias as can an operational data base.

Another problem with external data bases is that they often contain a sparcity of information—the detailed data elements that are often found in operational data bases are often missing. This limits the ways the data can be viewed. By definition external data bases are dated. They can be no more current than to the moment they are made available to the end user for processing.

Often a shop will lease or purchase an external data base for a specific need, only to find that multiple end users can use the data. As a regular matter of course when an external data base is acquired, the organization should make the acquisitions public knowledge so that the full benefit of the external data base can be realized.

The worth of external data bases can be measured in several ways. One way is to estimate the worth of having the external data base versus not having it at all. In this case the effectiveness of the external data is measured indirectly by the rise or fall of prosperity indicators. Another measure of worth is to calculate the costs of acquisitions of the external data base versus the costs of otherwise deriving the data base, or even acquiring the data base from another source.

External data bases are often found in organizations concerned with direct distribution, such as financial institutions, marketing firms, and public relations.

PROTOTYPING

Because of the flexibility and ease of construction, end user tools are ideally suited for prototyping operational systems. When, in gathering requirements, a user gets stuck in the "give me what I say I want, then I will tell you what I really want" mode, the ability to produce prototyped screens and reports can be a godsend. The major pitfall with end user computing tools for prototyping occurs when the user has finished the formal system requirements and assumes that the prototyped system is in fact, the finished system. The very flexibility of end user tools entails overhead that, under a high volume of data and/or transactions, makes the tools unsuitable (or at the least, inefficient) for operational systems.

The user who is building requirements through prototyping must understand that when the requirements are finally completed, the real system must be constructed. Nevertheless, the number of reiterations of building system requirements makes them well worth the effort.

Prototyping is generally found in mature organizations with a large number of systems where the company is trying to reduce application development costs. Prototyping is generally done in a joint effort between data processing and the end user.

The worth of prototyping is difficult to directly measure. The best measure is the long-term measurement of expenditures of data processing. But this measure may be (in fact, probably is) subject to many variables, only one of which is the prototyping activity. Another measure may be the development cost per system, but this measure is likewise subject to many variables. Perhaps the best measurement (which undoubtedly is somewhat subjective) is the measurement of maintenance and system "touch-ups" required for prototyped systems.

ARCHIVAL PROCESSING

There is a fine line of distinction between archival processing and end user computing. Indeed, in some cases end user computing may be done on archival data. The question of whether processing is end user or archival becomes one of degree. If moderate amounts of historical data are being processed, then that processing may well fall in the domain of end user computing. But if massive amounts of archival data are being processed, then the processing is probably best classi-fied as archival processing. Archival processing is generally done on very large amounts of historical data, stored at a detailed level in an unstructured fashion. Archival data is stored for unknown future uses, whereas end user computing data is stored with at least a general understanding of the usage of the data.

The physical manipulation of archival data presents its own peculiar problems. Because of the amount of data (which is usu-ally considerable) and the length of time it is to be stored (which is likewise considerable), the cost and reliability of the media become an issue. One popular media that is cheap and reliable is microfiche. But once data has been stored on microfiche, it is not easily converted to a machine-readable format. This is fine as long as there is only a need to get at individual pieces of data stored on microfiche, but if there ever is a need to get at large amounts of data stored on microfiche, then it is painful to have to convert the data back into an electronically oriented media.

The tools of end user computing are peculiarly suited to most archival processing, since archival processing can be handled by set-at-a-time processing and because archival processing does not normally entail response-oriented process-ing.

Because of the size of and complexity of data, archival pro-cessing is generally initiated by data processing personnel. Once the data has been refined to a point where it is not un-wieldy, the end user is given the data and is free to manipulate it as desired. Archival processing is generally done in either a re-active or a proactive mode. It is common to find much archival data in regulated industries. In nonregulated industries some amount (which is considerably less than that found in regulated industries) of archival data is common.

The worth of archival data is often noncalculatable. In the case of regulation, archival data may be necessary to continue doing business. In other cases, the worth of archival data can be measured indirectly by the worth of the living sample and/or demographic data bases it supports.

USES OF END USER COMPUTING—
A BROAD PERSPECTIVE

An interesting perspective of the different uses of end user computing is shown by Figure 5–1. In this figure the different kinds of end user computing are classified according to their applicability toward efficiency or effectiveness (i.e., their orientation toward usefulness in the DP arena or the business arena).

Prototyping is unquestionably an activity directed toward the efficiency of processing (both the efficiency of development and the efficiency of operation). Trend analysis, when run on a regular basis, is also directed at efficiency. However, trend analysis can also be effectively used as a tool for making business

---

F   I   G   U   R   E   5-1

Computing Activities Related to Effectiveness and Efficiency

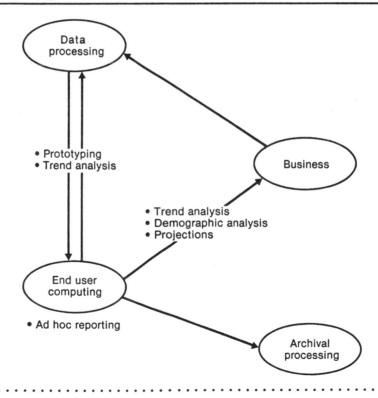

decisions. Demographic analysis and projections also are types of processing addressed primarily at business effectiveness. The only activity that can probably be classified as purely end user computing, in and of itself, is ad hoc reporting. In this sense, ad hoc reporting can be considered a primitive form of trend analysis, prototyping, or other forms of end user computing. Finally archival processing is a close cousin to end user computing. Archival processing uses tools and techniques found in end user computing, and in that regard may be considered to be a separate form of end user computing. But archival processing usually entails much more data than does traditional end user computing. Also, archival data is stored for future unknown needs, and end user computing has more structure and intent.

DIRECTIVES AND DIRECTIONS

- Trend analysis requires data that is "frozen" periodically. The freezing of data occurs as a result of an extract of production data.
- Trend analysis can be done on a regular basis or an ad hoc basis. When done on an ad hoc basis, the granularity of the data that has been frozen—the level of detail for a specific period—determines how many different ways the data can be analyzed. The finer the detail and the shorter the time span, the more ways the data can be analyzed.
- Ad hoc reports are usually run on data derived from production data, rarely from the production data itself. Ad hoc reports generally form the basis for "what if" analysis that is run as a series of iterated ad hoc reports, with limited changes from one report to the next.
- A living sample data base can greatly reduce the resources required to perform end user/decision support processing without affecting the validity of the processing.
- An unusually effective form of end user computing is demographic analysis, where end user tools are used to analyze a population base in the likelihood of directly increasing the marketing base.

- Models or spreadsheets are a form of end user computing that is forward looking, as opposed to trend analysis and other forms of end user computing that operate on data that describes past events. The algorithms and initial parameters form the backbone of spreadsheet processing.

An End User Computing Architecture

At the end of the month we add up profits and losses by line of business, by marketing division, and by geographic region. When you sum the numbers if they only differ by $2,000,000, it is a small miracle.

The fruits of an architected end user computing environment include consistency and believability of numbers, the ability to move the numbers through all systems in a short amount of time, reconciliation of any discrepancies, quick online response time, and the ability to look at end user computing data in multiple ways, as desired.

Architecting the DSS Environment

• •

The processing that occurs in most DSS environments is separated from the operational (or production) processing because of the different resource requirements of the two environments. The needs of DSS processing are dominated by:

Highly flexible data use.

Data at a summarized level.

Redundant data.

Data that represents the world from a "snapshot" perspective.

On the other hand, operational processing is dominated by a need for:

Highly structured data use.

Data at a detailed level.

Data that is accurate up to the second.

Nonredundant data.

For the shops that do very small amounts of processing on small amounts of data, there may be no need to separate operational and decision support processing. But when the processing requirements or the data requirements grow to any size at all, the processing needs are so diverse that physically separate processors are used. Such an environment, sometimes called a "dual data base" approach, can be physically separated as shown by Figure 6–1. The two physical configurations shown in the figure indicate that the operational environment is run on a mainframe, and the DSS environment is run on either a mainframe or a collection of microprocessors.

When DSS processing is done on a mainframe, it is usually done in a mode called the information center or the time-sharing mode. In the information center mode, the mainframe processor is divided into multiple private partitions, each one owned by a different user. As a user needs data, data bases are allocated to that user's private partition. Figure 6–2 depicts such a partitioning of the mainframe. In many ways the partitioning of users on a mainframe into private spaces and the allocation of data bases by users is the equivalent of many microprocessor users linked together on the same machine (i.e., the mainframe user partition is equivalent to a microprocessor in many ways).

F I G U R E   6–1

Two Most Common Operational/DSS Configurations

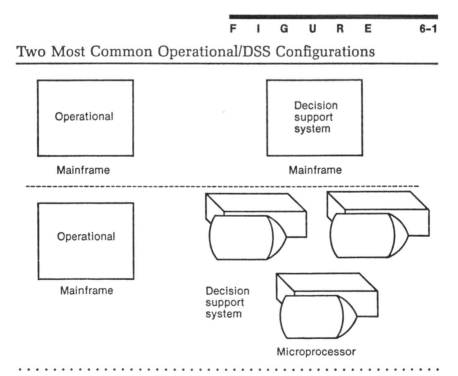

When a mainframe is used for DSS processing, it is often divided into partitions, which insulate the processing and data of one user from another. Each partition is roughly equivalent to the user operating on a microprocessor. Such a usage of a mainframe is often referred to as "information center" usage.

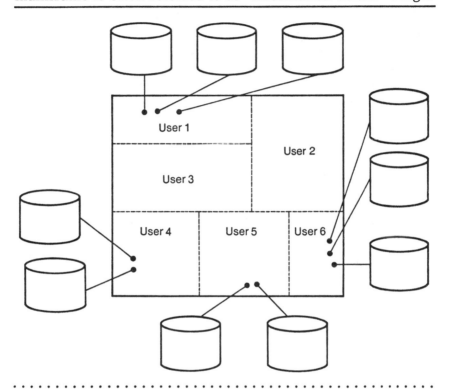

DATA EXTRACTS

The two environments—the DSS and the operational—are generally connected by a flow of data, usually from the operational to the DSS environment. The flow of data is termed "an extract." The term *extract* stems from the nature of the processing that connects the two environments. Operational data is scanned; data is selected and written onto an external media; the extracted data may (or may not) be sorted; and then it is passed to the DSS environment. If there is a need for character conversion as the data goes from one environment to the next, the conversion is usually done prior to the end user's reception of the data.

As long as there are very few operational and/or DSS data bases, a simple extract philosophy is quite adequate to interface the operational and DSS environments. In such a philosophy, operational data is simply scanned and directed to the DSS environment on an as-needed basis. Figure 6–3 depicts a simple scan and extract program. The data selection algorithm might be as follows: Look at every operational record. If the record is older than September 10, 1985, do not write to DSS data. Otherwise write the record to DSS data.

Large-Volume Environments

In the face of more than a few operational and DSS data bases, many problems arise with the simple extract approach to the interfacing of the operational and DSS environments. Two problems become more exaggerated the more frequently extracts are done. These problems are:

The resources needed to do many extracts.

The lack of synchronization or consistency of data and processing from one DSS data base to another.

F   I   G   U   R   E   6–3

Simple Scan and Extract Program

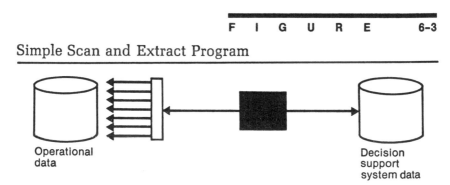

Operational data

Decision support system data

The scan program reads the entire operational data base and selects data for removal to the DSS environment. Sometimes this processing is referred to as taking a "snapshot."

Figure 6–4 illustrates the two major problems of a simple extract philosophy when applied across *many* operational and DSS data bases. Figure 6–4 shows that the same operational data bases are being scanned many times—in fact, the more DSS data bases there are, the more operational extracts are required. Not only is this wasteful of resources in general, but it is wasteful of operational resources in particular, which represent a very precious resource.

The second difficulty with a simple extract philosophy in the face of many operational and many DSS data bases is the lack of consistency of results that are achieved in DSS processing. Figure 6–4 shows that the same operational data base is

F   I   G   U   R   E   6-4

The Problems of Resource Utilization and Consistency of Data

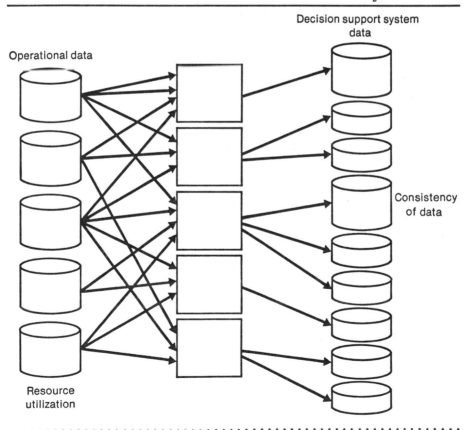

used as a source for multiple DSS data bases, but the same extract program is not used to deliver the data to the DSS data bases. Different selection, summarization, and merger logic is found throughout all the extract programs.

Inconsistent DSS Data

It is no wonder that the processing done by DSS data bases is inconsistent. If the processing and data are inconsistent, it is no surprise at all that the decisions resulting from the processing of DSS data are likewise inconsistent. Even if all the operational extract algorithms were identical (or at least resolvable), there would still be a problem in the timing of the running of the extracts. When an extract of an operational data base is done at 10 A.M., it is not surprising that the extract produces different results from one done at 4 P.M., since the operational data base is constantly being updated and undoubtedly will have changed from 10 A.M. to 4 P.M. Thus timing of extract processing, as well as the algorithm for extraction, is a necessary consideration when coming to grips with the issue of data consistency.

There is a further difficulty with the simple extract philosophy. It is normal for extracted data to be further refined and extracted for many iterations, as shown by Figure 6–5. The figure shows that extracted DSS data has the tendency to be further and further extracted, and each extraction and refinement further lessens the chance for data consistency. Thus it is no wonder that there is little consistency or consensus of opinion in DSS processing. In light of the problems caused by a simple extract philosophy, it is totally understandable why the DSS support from accounting may give completely different results than the DSS support from marketing (for example). Even when the two DSS support groups start with the same operational data, there is no reason to expect them to achieve consistency given the lack of discipline inherent to the simple extract philosophy carried to its normal conclusion. Furthermore, the more DSS users there are, the worse the problems of resource utilization and data inconsistency become.

Another major problem with the simple extract approach in the face of many DSS and operational data bases is that data continues to be extracted well beyond the operational/DSS interface, further diluting the consistency of the data.

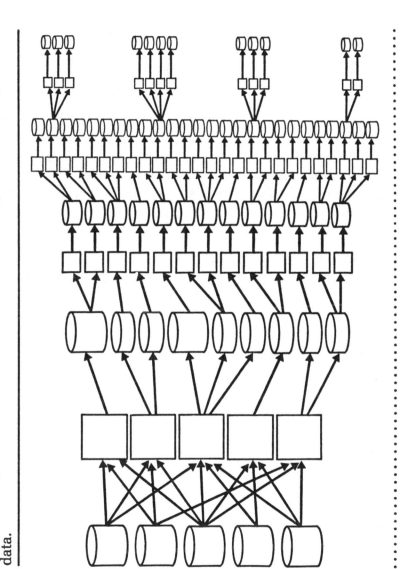

ARCHITECTING THE DSS ENVIRONMENT

The problems of the simple extract environment can be overcome. The solution is to "architect" the DSS environment. The building of an architecture and the discipline required to put and keep the architecture in place run contrary to one of the foundations of the DSS environment—the autonomy of the end user. The early selling of the DSS environment was based (at least in part) on the freedom end users enjoyed in building their own systems, but the end users' freedom collectively resulted in an uncontrolled, complex, expensive mess when multiplied by many users. (See Figure 6–6.) Thus it is that to be successful the architecting of the DSS environment requires a psychological shifting of gears by the end user as well as an understanding of the architectural framework.

Purpose of an Architecture

The two major problems of the simple extract environment then that need to be addressed by the architecting of the DSS environment are:

Resource utilization.

Data consistency.

A DSS architecture can effectively address these issues by entailing:

A single extract of any given operational data base for all DSS needs.

A single, controlled source for DSS data, from which inconsistencies can be resolved.

The architected DSS environment can be achieved by organizing DSS data into different levels and types. The architected levels of data include:

Atomic level.

Departmental level.

Individual level.

Flow of Data in an Architected DSS Environment

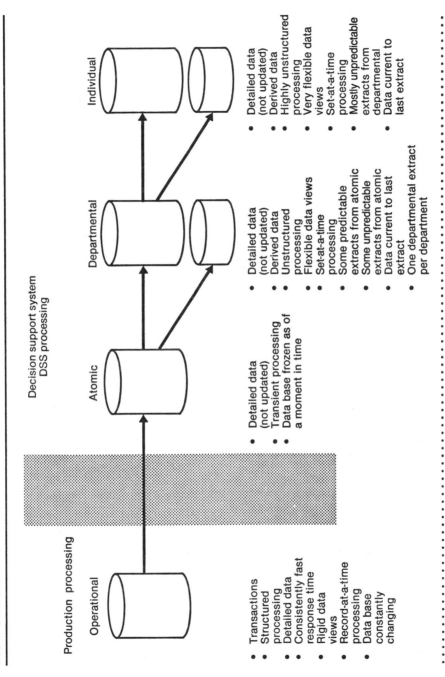

Production processing

Decision support system
DSS processing

Operational

- Transactions
- Structured processing
- Detailed data
- Consistently fast response time
- Rigid data views
- Record-at-a-time processing
- Data base constantly changing

Atomic

- Detailed data (not updated)
- Transient processing
- Data base frozen as of a moment in time

Departmental

- Detailed data (not updated)
- Derived data
- Unstructured processing
- Flexible data views
- Set-at-a-time processing
- Some predictable extracts from atomic
- Some unpredictable extracts from atomic
- Data current to last extract
- One departmental extract per department

Individual

- Detailed data (not updated)
- Derived data
- Highly unstructured processing
- Very flexible data views
- Set-at-a-time processing
- Mostly unpredictable extracts from departmental
- Data current to last extract

The different types of data within each level include:

Detailed data.
Derived data.

A detailed explanation of the different levels and types of data within each level follows.

ATOMIC DSS DATA

Atomic DSS data flows directly from the operational environment; it is stored at the most granular, detailed level appropriate to the DSS end user. Data at the atomic level is nonredundant across all other atomic DSS data except for foreign key values that are used to interrelate atomic data bases.

The granularity of atomic DSS data is important because it allows the data to be reshaped as desired by the end user. This allows the end user to achieve a high degree of flexibility. The nonredundancy of the data throughout the atomic level is important because it allows data to be reconciled, should there be any problems with consistency. It represents a moment at which the data is "frozen," something that doesn't exist with standard operational data bases. The redundant existence of foreign key values is important because of the relational join processing possible. Figure 6–7 depicts an atomic DSS data base extract.

Atomic—Operational Extract

Notice that any given occurrence of operational data is directed to only one atomic data base. This has the effect of greatly reducing the amount of processing done in the operational environment (thus satisfying one of the goals of an architecture—reduced resource consumption in the operational environment). At the same time, once the atomic DSS data bases are created, there is a single source for all other DSS processing (thus satisfying the second goal of the architected DSS environment—the achievement of consistency of data values). The extract shown in Figure 6–7 shows that different operational data bases are being extracted. If the operational environment is

Disciplined Extract of Data from the Operational Environment into Atomic DSS Data Bases

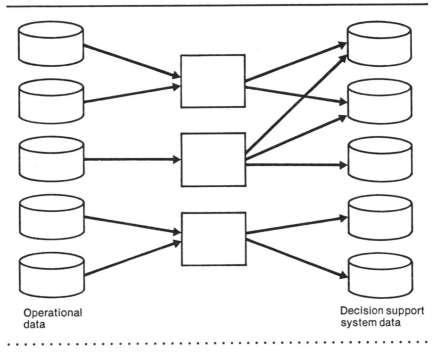

Operational data

Decision support system data

shaped around subject data bases, then there is a natural 1:1 correspondence between the operational environment and the DSS environment. Otherwise the correspondence is not 1:1. Also notice that there is nonredundancy of nonkey DSS atomic data. This point is worth illustrating with an example as it is not easy to see and is nontrivial. Figure 6–8 shows that at the operational level there is a single source of information—inventory activity. The different components of inventory activity are divided between stored DSS atomic data, work-in-progress DSS atomic data, and shipments DSS atomic data. Every unit of data from the inventory activity data base that is selected goes to one and only one DSS atomic data base. Thus the contents of the three DSS atomic data bases do not overlap, and taken together represent the totality of the operational inventory activity data that is selected for DSS processing.

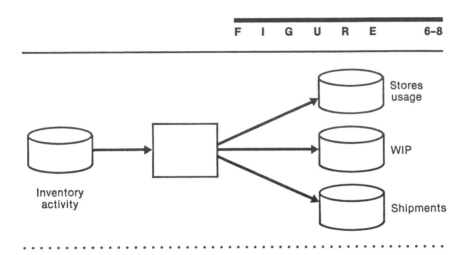

An extract program may select data from more than one operational data base to go into an atomic DSS data base, as shown by Figure 6–9. The figure shows that operational auto assembly, truck assembly, and motorcycle assembly data are extracted and are placed into a shop floor/plant floor control data base. Note that no other extract from the operational to the DSS environment may transfer the same data to the DSS environment.

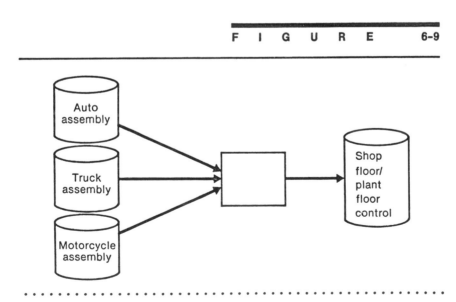

Suppose that in examining detailed data in the DSS environment an error or omission is spotted. The correction of the error takes place back in the operational environment and is reextracted into the atomic environment.

Given relatively small data bases, the approach of entire replacement (a refreshment) of data from operational to atomic, atomic to departmental, and so forth is optional. Wholesale refreshment of data ensures the most amount of accuracy with the least amount of complexity, but the total processing requirements of a refreshment approach can become very expensive in the face of any volume of data.

Another approach, in the face of volumes of data is the "appendage" philosophy. The appendage approach causes selected records—such as current activity and updates—to be shifted from operational to atomic, atomic to departmental, and so on. As the records are shifted, they must be inserted in the appropriate place. The appendage approach moves much less data but requires slightly more complex logic for the insertion of data.

A third approach is in the selective replacement of records. In this case only a very few records are selected for transfer from the operational to atomic, atomic to departmental, and so on. Upon arriving at the environment to be inserted, the record replaces an existing record, if in fact there is a corresponding existing record. The selective replacement approach moves even less data than does the refreshment or appendage approach but requires more logic to maintain the data. The trade-off in the maintenance of atomic, departmental, and individual end user computing data bases becomes one of volume of data versus complexity of processing. The purpose of the atomic DSS data bases is to serve as a common basis for all DSS processing. As such the DSS atomic data bases probably exist on a separate processor from the operational data bases.

DEPARTMENTAL DATA BASES

Departmental data bases are those that satisfy the needs of the department and are fed directly from (and only from) atomic data bases. There is a single departmental extract for each department. Each department must extract *all* the DSS data that

How Extracted Data Can Lead to Conflicting Conclusions

The three primary reasons the same source of data may not yield consistent results in the face of extract and derivation processing.

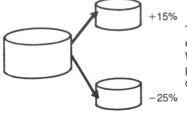

+15%

−25%

Timing — one extract was made on Sunday evening and the other extract was made on Wednesday afternoon. In the meantime, the production data base has undergone significant changes.

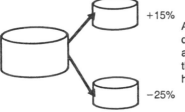

+15%

−25%

Algorithmic differences in the extraction and derivation process — one extract has selected accounts where the balance is over $100 and the other extract has selected accounts that have more than three pieces of activity per month.

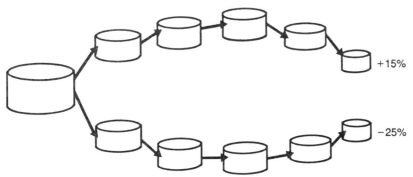

+15%

−25%

Generations of extracts — if there were a finite, limited number of extracts, comparison of any two might not be difficult. But it is common practice to have extracts of extracts. Furthermore, data may enter the generations of extract process randomly and may not be traceable in any case.

will be needed to suit its entire department's needs. As a department extracts data, some refinement and summarization is usually done. (Note: In small to mid-size corporations, departmental differences usually delineate different functional areas of processing. In the case of large corporations, major functional areas of processing may be spread over multiple departments. In this case, departmental data bases—as discussed—are really functional bases.) Whereas DSS atomic data is nearly all detailed, there is a mixture of detailed and derived data at the departmental level. Figure 6–10 illustrates an atomic to departmental extract in which detailed and derived data are mixed. The figure shows that the production control DSS department has extracted work-in-progress detailed data from the WIP DSS atomic data base. Included in this extract is much of the same detail as exists in the WIP data base. But as the detailed extract is done, parts usage summarized by month is calculated. The summarized-by-month data is a form of derived data, since its source of derivation is the detailed departmental data.

Another salient point is that among departmental data bases there is redundancy of nonkey data. Figure 6–11 shows such a case. In the figure production control DSS data and marketing DSS data are redundant in many cases. In some cases the selection algorithm may not be the same; in other cases it will be the same. If there is a need to reconcile marketing and production control differences, there are only two algorithms to be considered and a single common source of data on which the algorithms operate. It is noteworthy, however, that if there are multiple needs for departmental DSS data, there is only one departmental extract. In other words there is nonredundancy of nonkey data *within* the departmental level. As in the case of atomic DSS data bases (in fact, *all* snapshot-type data bases) the departmental data base is up to date only to the moment the extract from the atomic data base is made.

As has been previously noted, the *only* source of data for departmental DSS data bases is the atomic data base. Operational data *never* flows directly into departmental DSS data bases. Also note that it is normal to refine data as it is collected from the atomic DSS level. This may mean refining data with "what if" values or values from other sources. For example, suppose

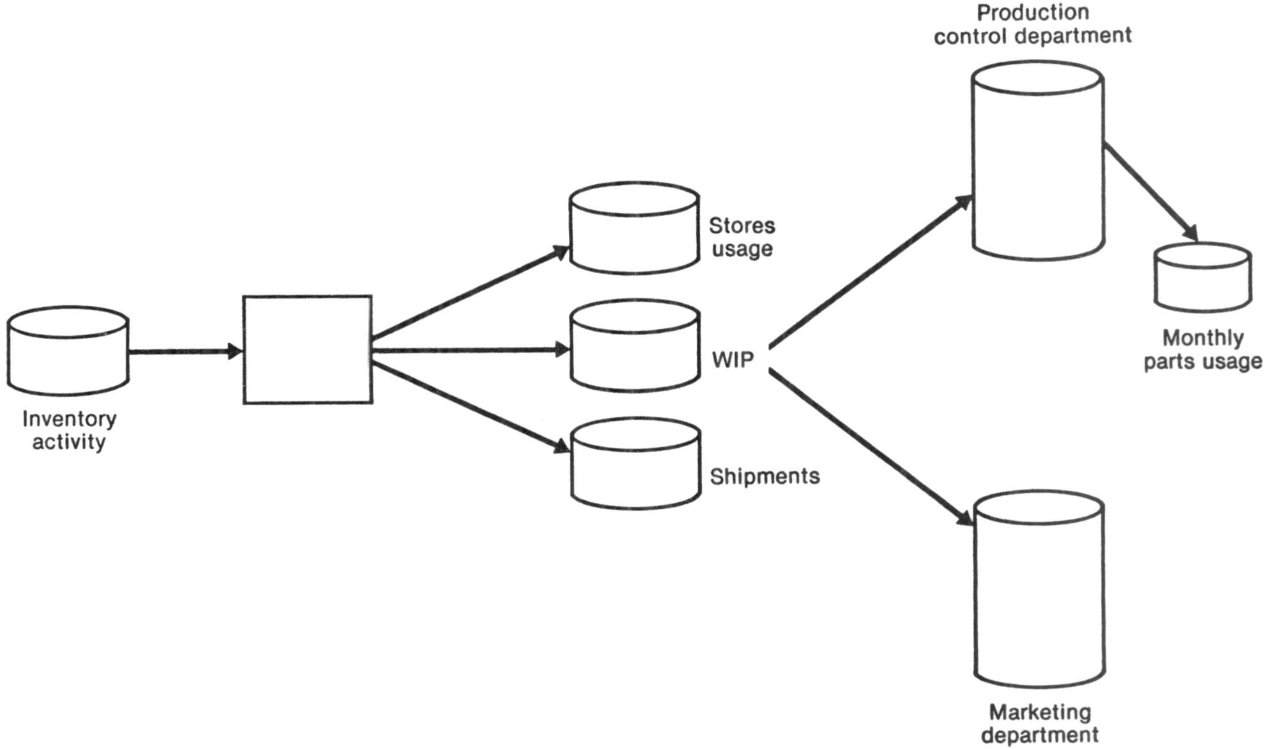

Production
control department

Monthly
parts usage

Marketing
department

Stores
usage

WIP

Shipments

Inventory
activity

FIGURE 6-11

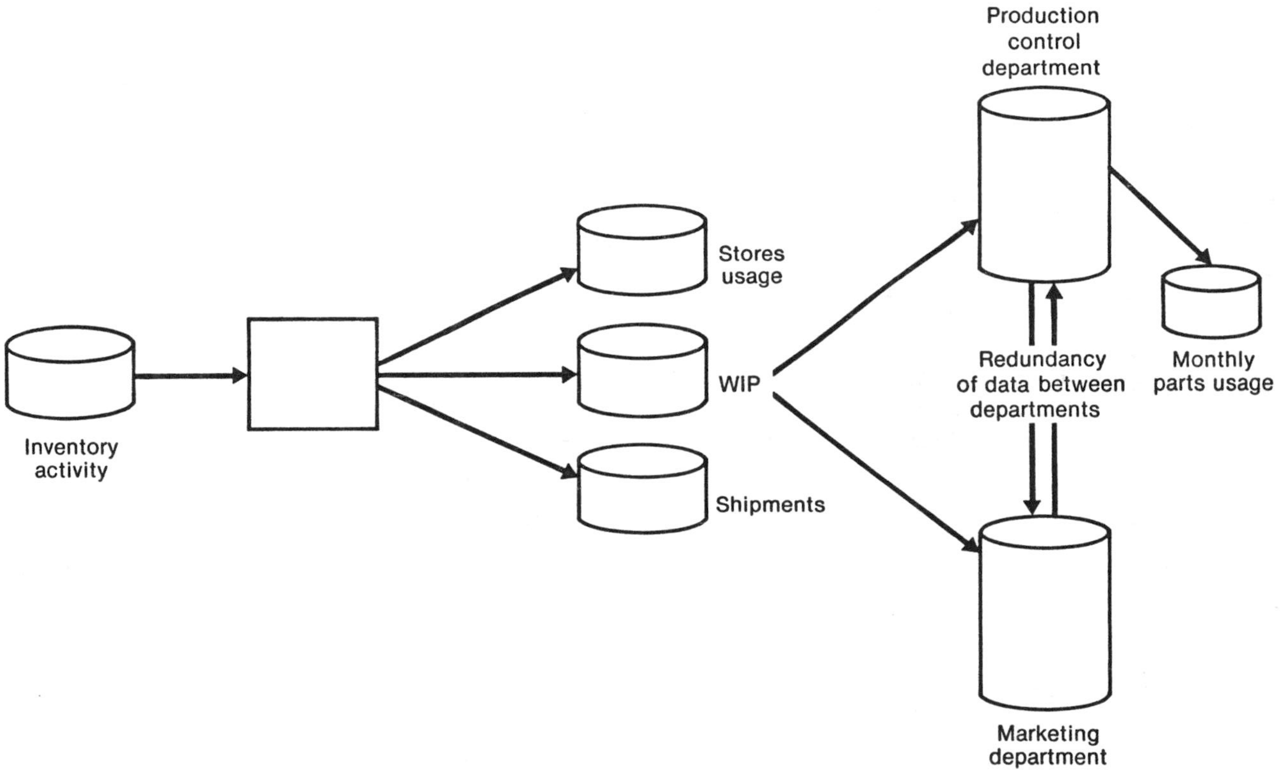

Production control department

Monthly parts usage

Redundancy of data between departments

Marketing department

Stores usage

WIP

Shipments

Inventory activity

that production data is extracted from the atomic DSS data base. A typical detailed unit of data might include part, finishing assembly, quantity, and so forth. From the standard costing file, the part and quantity can be "costed." In other words, the part is located in the costing file, its unit cost is determined, and the unit cost is multiplied times the quantity produced. Thus detailed data can be refined.

For derived data at the departmental level, updates may be needed. For example, suppose monthly production is stored by part. If adjustments need to be made at the monthly summation level, the update of data takes place at the departmental level. However, as in the case of atomic DSS data bases, if an error is found at the detailed level, then the correction must be made in the operational environment.

INDIVIDUAL DSS DATA BASES

The third level of DSS data is the individual level. The individual level is fed directly and only by the departmental level of data. Although the departmental level contains a combination of both detailed and derived data, the individual level contains almost exclusively derived data.

There is, generally speaking, much data redundancy between individual end users. Individual users extract data for each individual data base. All end users for a given department extract from the same departmental data base, although refinements to the individual data extracted may be done from various sources. It is at the individual level that most analysis is done. "What if" questions, trend analysis, demographic determination, projections—are all made here. Analytical activities may occur occasionally at other levels, but it is at the individual level that the bulk occurs.

THE DIFFERENT LEVELS

The progression from the atomic level to the individual level brings several issues to the surface. One issue is regularity of extracts. The atomic extracts (i.e., from the operational to the atomic) are done on a regularly scheduled basis; the individual extracts (i.e., from the departmental to the individual) are done on an as-needed basis; and the departmental extracts are somewhere in between. Furthermore, the extracts must reflect the totality of the needs served by the data. In other words, the operational to atomic extract must serve all DSS needs, the atomic to departmental must serve all departmental needs, and so forth. In this view the operational to atomic extract is probably designed and written by data administration. The departmental extract is created by a departmental analyst, and the individual extract is made by the individual analyst.

Another issue is data privacy. The scope of atomic data usage is very wide—covering *all* DSS users. Atomic data is public data—public to *all* DSS users. As the data progresses to individual usage, it becomes increasingly private. The scope of individual data use is *much* less than that of atomic data.

Given the tools of end user computing, it is normal to expect end users to build what are essentially classical operational systems at the individual level. There is nothing wrong with these systems, as long as:

They are economically justified.

The systems do not build or otherwise manipulate public data.

In other words, if the individual end user can cost justify systems and build systems that have no relevance outside of the end user's need, then there is absolutely no reason operational systems cannot be built at the individual end user level.

Another large issue is: Are three levels of DSS data proper for all organizations? For a really small organization, it may be appropriate to have just an atomic level and an individual level. For really large organizations, four or more levels may be appropriate. For most organizations, three levels are adequate.

Detailed/Derived Data

DSS data is classified first by different usage levels and second by types of data within levels. Figure 6–12 illustrates the percentage of data that would be expected to be found at each level. At the atomic level, data is nearly all detailed. At the departmental level, data is about evenly divided between detailed and derived data. And at the individual level, data is primarily derived.

Approximate Percentages of Data Expected at Each Level

	Atomic	Department	Individual
Detailed	99%	50%	5%
Derived	1%	50%	95%

Organizational Implications

The architecture for the DSS environment just described has a certain amount of appeal from a managerial and technical perspective. But it is a sure bet that implementation of the architecture described will encounter organizational resistance. The resistance stems from:

Change. Any change in work patterns encounters resistance.

Organizational boundaries. An implication of the architecture is that similar analytical activities stem from the same source of data. Organizations engaging in similar analytical activities may well be organizationally disconnected and have no intention of coordinating or combining efforts from a commonly shared departmental data base.

Autonomy. The essence of the end user environment is to "do your own thing." An architecture superimposed over the DSS environment requires a psychological realignment that may not be welcome.

Despite the factors that lead to organizational resistance (many of which are parochial, are self-serving, and represent a "local" perspective), there are plenty of overriding incentives to create and maintain the architecture (most of which stem from a mature, "global" perspective across the entire organization).

THE HARDWARE PERSPECTIVE

At the beginning of Chapter 6 two hardware environments were mentioned that were possible for the DSS environment— the mainframe environment and the microprocessor environment. The architected DSS environment at the individual level can fit in either mainframe or micro environment, but probably fits best in the microprocessor environment for the following reasons:

There is a limited amount of data for each end user in the architected DSS environment at the individual level.

Despite the physical limitations of the microprocessor environment, the microprocessor lends itself to very individualized processing, which is coincidentally supported by the architecture beyond the departmental level.

Because of the physical limitations of the microprocessor environment, the end user doing individual processing is not tempted to do departmental or atomic-level processing. In the mainframe environment, the end user may on occasion face this temptation.

In the architected DSS environment, there is a minimal need to share individual data, something reinforced by the individual microprocessor environment.

At the departmental level, because of the volume of data to be handled, it is unlikely that a microprocessor will suffice. Instead the departmental DSS level data is probably best handled by a minicomputer or small mainframe. And the atomic level, because of even more processing, is best served by a mainframe (or very large minicomputer). At the individual level there is most likely a processor per individual user. At the departmental level there is a minicomputer per department (i.e., it is unlikely that departments will desire to share the same processor with other departments). And at the atomic level there is a central processor (or complex of processors) that serves all atomic needs.

Another hardware issue is that of compatibility within each level. For operational systems it is desirable (but not necessarily mandatory) that all operational processors and software be compatible. For atomic-level data and processing, it is mandatory that all atomic-level data be compatible. For department-level data, it is unnecessary for different departments' data and processing to be compatible, even though there are some econo-mies of scale and consolidation to be enjoyed if the departments do in fact share compatible equipment. And at the individual level, it is unlikely that there will be a high degree of compatibil-ity of hardware and software.

Migratory Nature of the Architected DSS Environment

An interesting aspect of the architected DSS environment is that, although an optimal environment can be identified, that environment does not have to be realized all at once. It is very normal to create the architected DSS environment one step at a time. Once the blueprint for the architected environment is cre-ated, the existing environment can be analyzed in light of the long-term plan. The analysis will determine what parts of the existing environment will serve as a foundation and what parts won't. For those parts that will serve as a foundation, changes will be identified. In any case, atomic data bases can be created without a foundation of subject data base-oriented operational data bases. Over time, the operational environment can be cre-ated or altered a piece at a time.

Given that the architecture can be realized in a migratory fashion, there is much more satisfaction than if the architecture were a binary choice—either all in place or not in place at all.

THE ARCHITECTED END USER COMPUTING ENVIRONMENT—A SUMMARY

Table 6–1 represents a matrix of the different characteristics that are likely to be found in an architected end user computing en-vironment.

DSS DB ARCHITECTURE—EXAMPLE

Discussions about an architectured DSS environment are all very interesting when discussed in the abstract, but to make the architectured DSS environment come alive requires a complete example. The following example, based on a manufacturing plant, will trace a single event that happens in the plant from its measurement in the operational environment throughout the different architectural levels of the DSS environment. By focusing on a single event and tracing it through the environments and levels of DSS data it travels through, the reader can compare and contrast the differences in the architected DSS environment. Information about the event—the completion of an assembly order—will be traced from the operational to the atomic DSS environment. From there it will be traced through the marketing and production management departments. From the different departments individual analysis will be traced.

Operational Environment

Processing. Order 263195 was received by assembly 415 at the Pontiac plant on June 25, 1986, at 5:15 P.M. Since it was a high-priority order, order 376124, which was then being assembled, had to be interrupted. Setup time was estimated to take 1.5 hours. The order was for part number QX135, which was for "selection shafts." The order required that three units of selection shafts be built. Twenty-five shaft assemblies go into each unit. The order was based on engineering spec 2625 and was a standard assembly. The order was received by assembly-line worker Jane Jensen. Once completed the assembly would be routed to go into part QX139, which is a manifold shaft.

The work commenced at 10:35 A.M. on June 26. It was completed at 2:13 P.M. on June 26. The units were inspected by Chuck Curtis, of quality control. No defective parts were detected. Once completed, the three units were routed to Cheryl Elson, of assembly line 617.

During the assembly 75 units of shaft assembly, 20 pounds of solder, 150 shaft housings, 16 yards of wire, and 2,000 assorted nuts and bolts were used. Upon receipt of the order, most of the material was in place. But a stocking of 100 shaft housings and 150 units of shaft assembly was required during the manufacturing process.

MIS, End User Computing Architecture

Characteristic	Operational	Atomic	Departmental	Individual
Redundancy (Vertical)	No redundancy as goal	None, strictly controlled	Controlled redundancy among departments	Redundancy, free-form usage
Redundancy (horizontal)	Yes	Yes	Yes	Yes
Responsibility for data content	Operational user	Systems	Departmental user/ systems	Individual user, analyst
Responsibility for physical stewardship	Systems	Systems	Systems	User
Processing characteristics: (Creation)	Transaction (system of record)	Batch loads/unloads	Selective batch scans	Transfer and or creation
(Usage)	Record at a time, detailed	Transient, value added	Ad hoc, et al., sets of records at a time, summarized	Variety (indeterminate)
Data structure	Normalized data base	Subject data base	Application data base clustered	Individual data bases
Users	Detailed operational	Programmer analysts (indirect)	Application analysts, (directly) end user	End users
Flexibility: (Structure)	Rigid	Rigid	Flexible, based on atomic data	Highly flexible, based on departmental

(Contents)	Moderate	Flexible	Highly flexible	Infinitely flexible
Typical hardware	Mainframe	Mainframe	Mf, mini, PC, LAN	Mf, mini, micro, LAN
Typical software	IMS, IDMS	IMS, IDMS, VSAM, common data management software	Wide range, within data architecture's approved list	VM/CMS, Rbase 5000, anything desired by end user
Communications	Tape, temp disk, high volume, short time frame	Tape, channels	Tape, channels	Tape, channels, floppies
Location:				
Short term	Central	Central	Central	Central/distributive
Long term	Migratory	Central	Migratory, business dependent	Central/distributive
Segmentation	Controlled across organization	Controlled within architecture	N/A	N/A
Data source	User	Operational	Atomic	Departmental
Parameters of satisfaction	Response time, availability, detailed accuracy of data	Completeness of data, organization of data	Flexible usage of data, reconcilability of data	Individual needs of data, user autonomy of processing
Nature of data	Detailed	Detailed, some derived	Detailed and derived	Primarily derived
Nature of processing	Online	Batch—massive data movement	Batch—selective data movement	Micro, interactive—varying types of processing

Recorded Activity. Because of the processing of order 263195, the following transactions were individually submitted to the production control operational systems.

1. Order 263195 received, June 25, 1986, 5:15 P.M., three units, Jane Jensen, QX135, high priority.
2. Order 376124 interrupted 10:35 A.M., June 26, 1.5 hours setup.
3. Order 263195 completed, June 27, 1986, 2:13 P.M.
4. Order 263195, assembly 415, no defects, Chuck Curtis, QC.
5. Inventory usage—75 units shaft assembly, order 263195, June 26, 1986.
6. Inventory usage—20 lbs. solder, order 263195, June 26, 1986.
7. Inventory usage—150 shaft housings, order 263195, June 26, 1986.
8. Inventory usage—16 yards wire, order 263195, June 26, 1986.
9. Inventory usage—2,000 assorted nuts/bolts, order 263195, June 26, 1986.
10. Order 263195 routed to assembly 617, Pontiac, accepted Cheryl Elson.
11. Warehouse issue—100 shaft housings, line 415, Pontiac, June 26, 12:31 P.M.
12. Warehouse issue—150 units, shaft assembly, line 415, Pontiac, June 26, 12:31 P.M.

ATOMIC DETAILED DBS

From the data in the operational environment the atomic DSS data bases are created by means of an extract. They are physically divided into different data bases, two of which are the inventory usage DSS data base and the parts activity data base. Logically of course the physical ones make up a single DSS data base centered around the basic corporate entity part. The inventory usage DSS data base contains information about inventory usage, and the parts activity data base contains information about the manufacturing activity of parts.

The inventory data base contains at the element level the part (as key), the units issued, the store the part was issued from, the date/time of issue, the quantity issued, and the line to whom the issuance was made.

The parts data base contains information about the work done on any assembly. The key of the data base is *assembly* (which is synonymous with *part*). Other elements include the date/time the order was complete, who (the initials) received the order, the quantity ordered, the unit of measure (if nonstandard), the date/time the order was received, the date/time the order was commenced, the identification of the inspector (if inspection was done), an indication if standard engineering specs were used, the identification of the engineering spec used if the spec was nonstandard, if the order interrupted another assembly order, the assembly order that was interrupted (if in fact an interruption occurred), the number of parts rejected (if any parts were rejected), and finally, the assembly the order is routed to next.

ATOMIC DETAILED FLOW

On June 28 an extract of production control data is done from the appropriate operational sources. This extract flows directly into the DSS atomic data bases. Included as individual units of data in the extract are:

Part Inventory Usage

Seventy-five standard units shaft assembly, order 263195, line 415, June 26, 1986.

Twenty pounds solder, order 263195, line 415, June 26, 1986.

One hundred fifty shaft housings, order 263195, line 415, June 26, 1986.

Sixteen yards wire, order 263195, line 415, June 26, 1986.

Part Warehouse Issue

One hundred shaft housings, line 415, Pontiac, June 26, 12:31 P.M.

One hundred fifty units, shaft assembly, line 415, Pontiac, June 26, 12:31 P.M.

Parts Activity

Assembly—QX135, assembly order—263195, line 415, Pontiac.

Date complete—June 26, 1986, time complete—2:13 P.M.

Received by—Jane Jensen, priority—high.

Quantity—3, U/M—standard.

Date order received—June 25, 1986, time received—5:15 P.M.

Date order commenced—June 26, 1986, order commenced—10:35 A.M.

Lot inspection—QC–cc, engineering spec—std., nonstd. engineering spec—xxxx.

Assembly interrupt—yes, interrupted assembly—376124.

Parts reject—0.

Routed into—617, Pontiac.

Note that *many* other units of data are extracted along with these units of data; but for the purpose of the example, attention is centered on the data that comes from the single event being measured. Also notice that the atomic data is nonredundant and is stored at the most granular level. This means that any user may resequence, refine, and so on in as many ways as the data can be refined. This results in as *high* degree of flexibility as can be attained.

The inconsistency of end user/DSS data is addressed by atomic data bases and an architected DSS environment in the following ways:

- If timing of extracts is the issue, then the atomic data base represents data that is "frozen" as of some moment. The atomic data base can be easily reset to a previous moment, and extract processing can commence as of that moment.
- If algorithmic inconsistency in the extraction and derivation of data is the reason inconsistency exists, then in

How Atomic Data Bases and an Architected Approach to the DSS Environment Address the Problems of Data Consistency

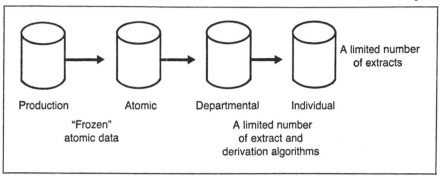

Production — Atomic — Departmental — Individual

A limited number of extracts

"Frozen" atomic data

A limited number of extract and derivation algorithms

an architected environment a minimum of algorithms must be resolved, and the algorithms are very visible and accessible.

- If the number of extracts and derivations is the reason for inconsistency, then the architected environment allows for only a limited number of levels of data, and there is no "foreign" entry of unresolvable data into the architecture.

MARKETING DEPARTMENTAL DETAILED, DERIVED DBS: A DESCRIPTION

All part activity for the detailed DSS departmental atomic data base flows directly from the associated atomic DSS data base. From the departmental data base, each part is assigned a certain set of values—a manufacturing value (i.e., what the part costs to manufacture times the unit manufactured), a wholesale cost (i.e., what the part wholesales for times the units manufactured), and the retail value (i.e., what the part retails for times the units manufactured). Note that value calculated is a marginal value—it applies to the incremental value the part adds to the total assembly. The values are derived through a standard set of costs/prices for each part in the bill of material.

The marketing trend data base is created monthly. After creation each part is passed against the bill of material to deter-

Marketing Department Data Bases

Part activity	Parts valued activity	Parts marketing trends
Part	Part	Part
Order number	Order number	Date completed
Date completed	Manufacturing value	Quantity
Time completed	Wholesale value	Unit
Quantity	Retail value	Expedite
Unit of measure	Quantity	Critical path?
Date order received	Unit	
Time order received	Date completed	
Date order commenced		
Time order commenced		
Expedited?	(Derived DSS	
Routed into	data bases)	
(Detailed DSS data)		

mine if the part is on the critical path or not. Given that sales are seasonal, certain parts are deemed to be on the critical path at different times of the year. The expedite field is used to signify whether or not each part/order has been expedited.

MARKETING DEPARTMENTAL DETAILED, DERIVED FLOW

On June 30, the marketing department commences to do some regularly scheduled analysis. First the marketing departmental detailed DSS data base is loaded from the atomic DSS data base. Note that there is a fair degree of stripping away of detail at this point. Next the "value" marketing data bases are loaded. These extracts and loads have the effect of loading the following data into the departmental data bases:

Part Activity

Part—QX135, order no.—263195.

Date complete—June 26, 1986, time complete—2:13 P.M.

Quantity—3, units—standard.

Order receive date—June 25, 1986, order receive time—5:15 P.M.

Order commence date—June 26, 1986, order commence time—
10:35 A.M.

Expedited?—yes, routed into—QX139.

Note that many other values relating to other activities than
the activity being traced are loaded at the same time.

Next the departmental part activity data base is passed with
valuing information for the activity being traced. The result is:

Parts-Valued Activity

Part—QX135, order no.—263195.

Date complete—June 26, 1986.

Quantity—3, units—standard.

Manufacturing value—10.75.

Wholesale value—24.50.

Retail value—46.50.

The data that has flowed to the marketing trend data base is as
follows:

Part—QX135, date—July 26, 1986.

Quantity—3, unit—standard.

Expedite—yes.

Initial path—yes.

MARKETING INDIVIDUAL DETAILED/DERIVED DBS

Once the marketing departmental data base is loaded, the individual marketing analysts can start to do their job. There are
several marketing DSS data bases that are created for individuals. Some of these data bases include the valued parts
data base, the adjusted valued parts data base, the monthly
summation of parts, and the monthly summation of expedited/
nonexpedited parts. The first data base describes valued parts
and the adjustment to those valued parts. The second data base
describes a readjustment of the values. Previous values are
saved for the purpose of comparison.

The first data base contains the summation by month of the different categories of data. The differences on a month-by-month basis can be compared. The next data base contains the summation by part for the month of the units that were expedited and the units that were not. In addition, it indicates whether or not the part was critical during the month. Note that at this point much of the information about the activity being traced is summed with other similar information. The unique identity of the information is lost at this point.

MARKETING INDIVIDUAL DETAILED/DERIVED FLOW

The president of the company engages a consulting firm to forecast future market conditions. The firm indicates that the price of basic steel is going down, but certain manufacturing processes will become more expensive due to the chemicals used in process. The firm also states that Japanese competition will cause the price of the end product to come under severe stress given current price levels.

The president of the company asks the marketing DSS organization to analyze the impact of these changes on the company. First the engineering bill of material is used to determine new steel price and new chemically related adjustments. This is use-

---

Marketing Department Individual DSS Data Bases

Parts value—analysis 1	*Parts value—analysis 2*
Part	Part
Date	Date
Quantity	Quantity
Unit of measure	Unit of measure
Manufacturing value	Manufacturing value
Wholesale value	Wholesale value
Retail value	Retail value
Manufacturing value—adjusted	Manufacturing value—adjusted
Wholesale value—adjusted	Wholesale value—adjusted
Retail value—adjusted	Retail value—adjusted
	Manufacturing value—readjusted
	Wholesale value—readjusted
	Retail value—readjusted

ful to determine cost changes on a unit basis, but it is not good for applying the changes across all units in manufacture. The president requests that the marketing DSS analysis group analyze actual production activities to further refine estimates. Using the valued parts DB, a new (revalued) parts data base is created. The president considers the results and begins to ask "what if" questions, such as: What if the price of steel doesn't drop, but the price of chemicals still rises? The revalued parts activity data is revalued once again. From a data perspective, for the activity being traced, the result is the creation of the following records:

Part revalued activities (analysis 1)	*Part revalued activity (analysis 2)*
Part—QX135, date—June 26, 1986.	Part—QX135, date—June 26, 1986.
Quantity—3, units—standard.	Quantity—3, units—standard.
Manufactured value—10.75.	Manufactured value—10.75.
Wholesale value—24.50.	Wholesale value—24.50.
Retail value—46.50.	Retail value—46.50.
Manufactured revalue—8.56.	Manufactured revalue—8.56.
Wholesale revalue—24.50.	Wholesale revalue—24.50.
Retail value 46.50.	Retail revalue—46.50.
	Manufactured rerevalue—13.61.
	Wholesale rerevalue—24.50.
	Retail rerevalue—46.50.

After the different value analyses are done, the cumulative effect of pricing is tallied, by all products, and by unit price for each end product. There are two data bases that are derived:

WIP parts	*End products*
Part	End product
Condition set	Condition set
Time span	Time span
Value	Value
.	.
.	.
.	.
.	.

Critical path order analysis	Part, month expedite analysis
Month (summed by month)	Part
Critical orders, expedited	Month
Critical orders, nonexpedited	Critical (y/n)
Noncritical orders, expedited	Units expedited
Noncritical orders, nonexpedited	Units not expedited

The work-in-progress data base values the actual work in progress according to different sets of conditions, as determined by the analyst. The end product data base, using the bill-of-material explosion, values the end product according to different condition sets. The output from different condition sets is saved so that different scenarios can be compared with each other. For the critical path order analysis, the order for part QX135 shows up in summation with all other critical, expedited parts for June. In the second critical path data base, the activity is summed with all other June activity for part QX135. The number of units—three—is summed with all other expedited units. Note that there is little identifiable unique data about the original event being traced that is discernible at this point. Most data has been summed or otherwise discarded.

PRODUCTION DEPARTMENTAL DETAILED, DERIVED DBS

The production management department regularly strips the DSS atomic data into its departmental data bases. Some of the data bases are as shown. As in the case of marketing departmental data, there is a difference between a logical data base and a physical data base. The production department recognizes a single logical atomic data base, based on part, that is manifested by multiple physical data bases. The physical data bases, taken in summation, form the logical atomic DSS data base. Shown in this example is one of those physical data bases.

Production Management Department DSS Data Bases

Order management

Order
Part
Line
Location
Date received
Time received
Date commenced
Time commenced
Date finished
Time finished
Expedite?
Interrupt?
Quantity
Unit of measure
Engineering spec
Parts reject

DEPARTMENTAL DETAILED, DERIVED FLOW

Production Management

The result of loading the order management departmental DSS data bases from the atomic is that the following (as one of many units) is loaded:

Part—QX135, line—415, location—Pontiac.

Date received—June 25, 1986, time received—5:15 P.M.

Date commenced—June 26, 1986, time commenced—10:35 A.M.

Date finished—June 26, 1986, time—2:13 P.M.

Expedite—yes, interrupt—yes.

Quantity—3, units—standard.

Engineering spec—standard.

Part reject—0.

As in the case of marketing departmental data, many other units of data not directly related to the event being traced are likewise extracted. Note that only relevant detail is stripped, and that at this point detailed data is the only type of data found.

PRODUCTION INDIVIDUAL DETAILED, DERIVED DBS— A DESCRIPTION

The first individual DSS data base—the process analysis data base—is for analyzing by line by month the length of time an order is processed. It is stored with other historical information by month. The average process time is the length of time from commencement to finish. The average elapsed time is the time from the receipt of order to finish. All types—process and elapsed—are summed and averaged over the month. The second individual DSS data base—the interrupt analysis data base—is collected by line by month and is stored with other historical data. The number of times a line was interrupted is summed by month. The third data base—the engineering spec analysis—is used to determine how often standard and non-standard specs are followed. The data is collected by line by month and is summed with other like data.

PRODUCTION INDIVIDUAL DETAILED, DERIVED FLOW

In the first individual DSS data base—the process analysis data base—part QX135 for June has its elapsed time calculated and summed and averaged with all other part data for the month. For the interrupt analysis data base, the part QX135 for June tallies +1 in the interrupt total, since order 376124 was interrupted. For the third data base, part QX135 for June tallies +1 in the standard engineering specification orders, since order

Production Department Individual DSS Analysis Data Bases

Process analysis	Interrupt analysis	Engineering spec analysis
Part	Line	Line
Month	Month	Month
Line	Interrupts (summed)	Standard spec orders (summed)
Average process time		Nonstandard spec orders
Average elapsed time		(summed)

263195 was a standard engineering specification order. Once these data bases are built, reports are run showing monthly results and a month-by-month comparison of totals. Note that the event being traced has lost much identity at this point. For the most part, the event exists as derived data or scanned data.

DATA FLOW THROUGH THE ARCHITECTED ENVIRONMENT

Figure 6–13 describes the flow from the operational environment to and throughout the architectured DSS environment. The flow from the operational environment is directly to the atomic DSS data bases. From the atomic data bases, departmental data bases are fed; and from the departmental data bases are fed the individual data bases.

The extract from the operational environment is at a very low level of detail. All DSS needs must be met from this extract. (Of course, the flow depicted in Figure 6–13 does not show *all* DSS data bases. Only those relevant to the example are included.) As data is extracted from one level to the next, the amount of detailed data lessens, and the amount of derived data grows. At the individual level wherein most of the analysis occurs, there is very little detailed data and much derived data. Note that in some cases detailed and derived data are mixed in the same data base, and in other cases detailed and derived data are not mixed but are explicitly stored separately. Also note that the total amount of data greatly diminishes in going from the atomic level to the individual level. It is not surprising that there is much detailed data and progressively less individual data.

The update of data that occurs in the DSS environment is exclusively that of derived data. For example, one month's worth of production data is stored (i.e., updated into a data base) with other months' worth of data. Any corrections are made against derived data at the point of derivation. If the corrections are for data directly derived from detailed data, then an audit trail must be kept showing when and how the derived data was altered.

Also note that the further away from the atomic level the data flows, the more summarized and refined it tends to be. Another observation is that the further DSS data base flows from

Flow of Data from the Operational Environment to and through the DSS Environment

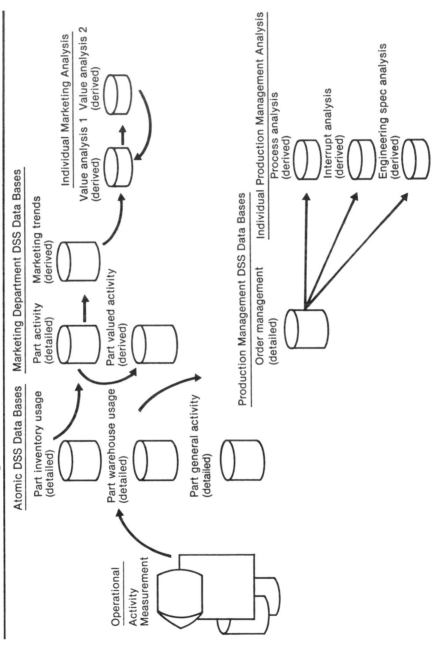

the atomic level, the less regularly scheduled processing (i.e., extract, analysis, etc.) is done. Indeed, most "what if" processing is done at the individual level of processing.

Another interesting point is that some data flow from one level to the next is regularly scheduled, and some flow is spontaneous. This irregularity of flow is necessary to achieve the flexibility of end user computing. Despite the irregularity of flow, considerations should be made for the volume of data that is flowing. For regularly scheduled flows of data, the amount of data flowing should be minimized. But for irregularly accessed data, it is usually necessary to scan entire atomic data bases. These scans will necessarily involve large amounts of data. The carefully architected end user computing environment then takes into consideration the fact that large amounts of data are involved, and there will occasionally be a need to scan all atomic data.

FURTHER CONSIDERATIONS OF THE MANUFACTURING ARCHITECTURED DSS ENVIRONMENT

The example of the manufacturing architected DSS environment serves to point out many details that are otherwise difficult to envision. Consider the following:

1. Suppose a research analyst while looking in the atomic DSS data base finds that line 904 has built 300 units of part ZX132, instead of 3 units of the part. The research analyst must go to the operational environment, make the correction to the data there and have the data reextracted. Consider what happens if the research analyst makes the correction to the detailed data in the DSS atomic environment. The correction is made, and ensuing DSS processing is correct but:

    • The operational environment is incorrect, and operational decisions are being made on data that is *known* to be inaccurate.
    • If further extracts are made from the operational environment, it is entirely possible that the DSS atomic en-

vironment will have correct data overlaid with incorrect data. Thus it is that when detailed errors are identified, the change must be made at the operational level (i.e., system of record).

2.   Suppose it is desired to do a special type of valuing processing in the accounting department. If there is to be any meaningful comparison of results to the existing analysis, *at the very least*, the raw data used to produce existing valuation must be used. In addition the valuation algorithm must be accounted for. But what if the valuation analysis is to be done by an entirely different department? The organizational implications are clear. If unified or meaningful comparisons are to be made, there are organizational issues that must be resolved, as well as technical issues.

SUMMARY

If there ever is to be consistency of data and processing in the end user computing environment, there must be a disciplined organized approach taken to creation and usage of end user computing systems. The architecture that results must take into account that:

Operational and DSS data have very fundamental differences.

Large amounts of data must be accounted for.

The achievement of end user flexibility is accomplished through controlled redundancy of data.

The resulting architecture will have, in one form or the other:

Different levels of data—atomic, departmental, and individual.

Different types of data within each level—detailed, derived.

The architecture that results requires change and organizational conformance, which is predictably resisted by the end user who is attracted to end user computing by the autonomy of processing.

DIRECTIVES AND DIRECTIONS

- The differences between operational and end user/ decision support data go well beyond the issue of system performance. The fundamental differences in the types of data include—

Level of detail—production data is detailed, end user data usually is summarized.

Usage of data—production data is used in a very structured fashion, and end user data is used in an unstructured fashion.

Timeliness of data—production data needs to be accessed up to the second, and end user data needs only to be accurate as of some moment in time.

Privacy of data—production data needs to be available across a wide network, and end user data needs to be available to a small private audience.

Availability of data—production data needs to be available continuously for long periods, and end user data needs to be available on an as-needed basis.

Rigidity of structure—production data tends to be inflexibly structured, and end user data tends to be structured very flexibly.

Intent of data—production data is used to run the enterprise, and end user data is used to manage the enterprise.

- The differences between production and end user data are such that separate data bases—"dual data bases"—are required.
- End user data is extracted and derived from production data.
- In the face of many end users and many end user data bases, the extraction and derivation process must be carefully architected.
- The three primary reasons end users using an extract and derivation process to retrieve end user data encounter a lack of credibility are (1) the timing of the extract

and derivation, (2) the differences between algorithmic selection and derivation, and (3) the complexity caused by generations of extracts and undisciplined sources of input.

- To achieve credibility in the decision support environment where there are many end users, much redundancy, and an extract and derivation process, the end user must be "staged" (i.e., exist at different levels). The different levels are (1) atomic end user level, (2) departmental end user level, and (3) individual end user level.
- Each data level has its own unique characteristics, and there is a disciplined flow of data from one level to the next.

CHAPTER 7

Executing the Architecture— Organizational Issues

● ●

The first major step in making the end user computing environment effective is establishing a computing architecture, as described in Chapter 6. Without a clearly defined architecture, it is very difficult to establish order. But the development of an architecture is meaningless unless it is manifested in terms of real systems and real uses. To use an analogy, an architecture is the equivalent of a blueprint, but a blueprint alone is fairly useless. Unless a foundation is built according to the blueprint, unless walls, roofs, and a building are constructed, the act of building a blueprint is futile. So it is with an end user computing architecture. The architecture must be executed for the results to be gleaned.

There are really two major perspectives to the execution of the end user computing architecture—that of the end user as the end user builds systems and the more global perspective of the organization as the architecture is executed. This chapter deals with the more global issues. Chapter 8 deals with the issues of executing the architecture from the individual end user perspective.

THE ORGANIZATION CHART

The first and most obvious necessity is some authoritative body within the organization that has jurisdiction across all end users as to the creation, manipulation, and usage of data found in the end user environment. Traditionally, this has meant the authoritative office is set high in the organization chart, where interorganization communication and control are natural and easy. Functionally, the job being done at the high organizational level is that of classical data administration. But traditionally data administration has been at a lower technoclerical level in the organization. For lack of a better term then, the position to be discussed will be *chief end user computing information officer,* or CIO.

It is the job of the CIO to serve as:

Creator and caretaker of the end user computing architecture (for hardware, software, and data).

Monitor of conformity to the architecture across the organization.

Court of last resort as to questions concerning the architecture.

A reference as to the proper usage of the architecture.

The CIO serves then as a liaison between upper management and the actual end user computing analysts. The CIO has architectural definition and conformance duties across *all* end user computing activities. The position of the CIO is greatly diluted if end user computing occurs that is not under the auspices of the CIO.

On the one hand, the CIO is charged with the conformance to the end user computing architecture. But merely having a watchdog function is insufficient. Impetus for conformance to the computing architecture must originate with the end users themselves. To be successful, end users give up some autonomy of processing, but the entire organization gains in effectiveness. Since there is naturally resistance to giving up autonomy, both top management and the CIO must carefully explain to each end user what the architecture is, why the architecture is important, and exactly what is meant by conformance. This is both an education and a selling process.

It is very questionable if the architecture will ever be properly executed if the CIO relies solely upon organizational position and authority. End user enthusiasm and compliance are at the heart of success. The role of the CIO in establishing the architecture is first to define the architecture, second to outline the steps in the execution of the architecture, and third to follow those steps. In addition the CIO must constantly update and revise the architecture.

ORGANIZATIONAL RESISTANCE

The CIO will first face resistance when introducing a limitation to the end users' autonomy, but other resistance will be encountered later. There will be resistance to the organizational position and role of the CIO. Most organizations are not used to organizational units that cross the entire company. Furthermore, the notion that end user computing data (and hardware and software) must be controlled and used in a disciplined fashion and that another organizational unit has an authoritative say is an alien concept.

Such resistance is fairly mild when compared with the resistance that occurs when the CIO states that two entirely separate departments must share data. Where two organizational units do similar or related functions, there is a need to have a single source for functionally similar data. But often two (or more!) departments that have an overlap in function are competitive with each other, and the last thing they want is the suggestion that there should be a consolidation of effort, even if the consolidation is only of data. From a departmental perspective, such an attitude is certainly defensible; but from a corporatewide perspective, such an attitude reflects organizational immaturity, and it is the job of the CIO to represent the corporatewide perspective.

The Role of the CIO

Thus it is that the CIO can anticipate huge amounts of resistance. For this reason it is imperative that the CIO:

Has the full understanding and support of top management.

Conditions the organization to the importance of an architecture as part of the execution of the architecture.

Has final authority and responsibility for the existence and flow of data throughout the end user computing environment. The CIO then represents the force for corporate discipline in the usage of end user computing. Of principle concern to the CIO are the data architecture, the flow of data, and the selection (and processing) algorithms as the data flows from the atomic to the departmental to the individual levels of processing. In addition, the CIO is concerned with the hardware and software found in the end user computing environment. However, the issue of hardware and software is almost always the first issue breached by the end user, and once decided, it is seldom revisited.

Documentation and the CIO

One of the cornerstones of CIO success is in the documentation of the architecture. As important as documentation is in the traditional DP department, documentation takes on an even more important role in the end user computing environment. If there ever is to be corporatewide control of the end user environment, there needs to be a clearly defined mission and explanation of the architecture and how it is to be executed.

End users cannot be blamed for nonconformance if they do not understand what the architecture is in the first place. Thus it is that the CIO needs to clearly identify and enunciate what the architecture is. The documentation of the architecture should *at the least* be:

Publicly available

Up to date

Complete

Easy to read

Indexed

Organized

At the very least, the documentation should include:

A definition and description of the atomic data.

A definition and description of the departmental data.

A definition and description of operational to atomic extract algorithms.

A definition of atomic to departmental extracts.

The high-level (ERD) view of the data.

The appropriate midlevel (dis) views of the data.

An identification of the operational source(s) of data.

The user views appropriate to the ERD.

The dimensions appropriate to the ERD.

Other Issues Facing the CIO

The CIO, once having defined and established the end user computing architecture, has the task of:

Consulting with end users as problems arise.

Relating corporatewide problems, successes, et al. to upper management on a periodic basis.

Periodically auditing end user computing.

Periodically updating the end user computing architecture.

Measuring insofar as possible the payback of end user computing.

Keeping public documentation up to date, accurate, and available.

Another issue facing the CIO is archival processing. What is to be actively kept in the atomic data bases? What data is to be discarded outright? What data is to be kept in archival files after it has left the computing environment? When is data to be archived?

These issues and more fall to the domain of the CIO and belong as a standard part of the end user computing architecture. It is noted that the tight control of the CIO ends at the departmental-atomic interface. Individual processing is still up to the individual analyst. Once having been directed to the proper data, the analyst has the freedom to process data as desired. The autonomy of processing of the end user is not lost at the individual level. There are, however, two issues that the CIO may wish to monitor in individual end user computing. The first issue is that of individuals building operational data bases when it would be more efficient to build them operationally or when there is public data involved. In this case, the end user needs to have the operational systems built in the traditional manner. The second issue arises when individuals are not using the proper data as a starting point for their processing. In this case, the CIO needs to direct the end user to the proper source(s) of data.

Although the CIO is essential in achieving an architected end user computing environment, another level of activity is also required. The CIO operates on a global, across-the-organization basis, but there is a need to assist and direct each end user computing effort on a day-to-day basis. It is at this level that traditional data administration functions best, sometimes in conjunction with the Information Center organization. At this level the data administration:

Directs and assists the end user in the location and access of data.

Conducts quality assurance reviews, verifying conformance to the architecture.

Aids in the reconciliation of data upon those occasions when inconsistent processing occurs.

Helps maintain architecture at the detailed level, including detailed documentation on a data dictionary.

Interfaces directly with the CIO concerning architectural issues.

Prepares estimates as to the impact of change.

Is heavily involved at the inception of projects.

Serves as the first-line, direct interface to the end user.

ARCHITECTURAL CONFORMANCE

There are three steps essential to the effective achievement of an architected environment:

The establishment of the architecture.

The conditioning of the organization to the architecture.

The actual conformance to the architecture.

From the perspective of the application developer then, what is meant by conformance to the architecture? How does a developer know when he or she has or has not conformed to the architecture? Following are some guidelines:

1. For operational and atomic processing, the system developer will not duplicate existing data or processes. If there is a need to use existing data or code, the developer will incorporate the existing data and code into the design. For end user computing data, there may be an overlap, especially of data, but even in that case, the overlap is controlled.

2. When a developer builds new data and processes, the general structure will conform to the architecture. Keys will be built for *all* usages—present and future—not just the immediate set of needs. Subroutines and common code will be built for *all* usages—present and future. The developer in essence builds systems with an awareness that future systems will be built on top of the immediate set of requirements.

3. The hardware/software that is chosen needs to be compatible with the architectural guidelines (i.e., the standard operating environment).

4. When new data is introduced into the systems built under the architecture, the data is first fit into the architecture, then is fit into the systems that are patterned after the architecture.

5. An essential component of the architecture is the differentiation between private data and public data. Private data is that that has no relevance beyond the immediate set of users building and manipulating data. Public data is data that does have usage, relevance, or other interest beyond the immediate set of users. All public data will conform to the architecture. Private data may or may not conform to the architecture, depending upon the wishes of the users.

6. At the implementation level, it is likely that data will be physically split (by key range, by geographic region, etc.). Splits will be made consistently across the architecture and all systems that are subject to the architecture.

7. The relationships that are defined across the architecture will be supported, even if the immediate set of processing requirements do not call for those relationships to be supported.

8. The high level overview and the specific details of the architecture will be made publicly available to anyone who wishes to peruse the architecture. The architecture will be kept up to date.

9. An essential component of the architecture is the deliberate separation of detailed, transaction-oriented processing and summarized, decision-support processing. A developer will be in clear violation of the architecture if the design that is developed is not in accordance with this separation.

10. All design, especially at the inception of the project, is subject to review, and if necessary, redirection by the architecture organization function (i.e., the CIO and/or data administrator).

SUMMARY

Building an architecture is only the first step in creating an effective end user computing environment. The execution of the architecture is the next necessary step.

Two organizational units must be established—at a high organizational level, the CIO; and at a lower, project level, the data administration organization. It must be recognized that resistance will appear in many forms for many reasons. As the CIO and data administration functions are established, there should be an awareness of the impending resistance.

A final issue is that of conformance to the architecture. As a major factor in reducing resistance, the requirements being placed on the end user to conform to the architecture need to be explicitly and publicly stated.

DIRECTIVES AND DIRECTIONS

- The first step in the architecting of the end user computing environment is establishing a blueprint; but to be effective, organizational changes must be made.
- There must be a "caretaker" (sometimes called a chief information officer) for the architecture. The caretaker is responsible for establishing and interpreting the architecture; crossing organizational boundaries to ensure the integrity of the implementation of the architecture; serving as a focal point for project-related data administration activities; providing feedback to upper management in regard to the successes and failures relaved to the architecture and its implementation; and overseeing the detailed day-to-day, project design decisions that relate to the architecture.
- To be successful the architecture must both be "sold" and enforced.
- The staffing of the caretaker function requires a blend of business skills and technical skills.

Developing the End User
Computing System

• •

Chapter 6 suggested that the most effective end user computing environments were carefully architected, and a prototyped architecture was proposed. Chapter 7 discussed the implementation of an end user computing architecture from the global, organizational perspective. Chapter 8 will now discuss the development of an end user computing system within the framework of an existing architecture. The issues of development will be discussed from the perspective of an individual end user.

There are many different pieces of end user software. Each has its own unique features—its own strengths and weaknesses, its own environments for which it is adapted. Rather than discuss end user computing system development from the perspective of one or more pieces of software, a more generic approach will be used. The reader will be guided through a sequence of issues, or considerations, that any end user must go through in order to develop an architected system. The approach will be to describe some general considerations that must have been satisfied to get to the next step. Any step-by-step description of a complex process becomes tedious and overworked, especially where there is a wide and diverse audience to be addressed and many design options that must be explored. The sequence of discussions and issues does not direct the end user in a how-to-do, cookbook fashion. Instead the reader will be subjected to a few criteria that must be met to go to the next level of development. *How* the end user computing developer satisfies those criteria is strictly up to the reader; *that* the developer satisfies the criteria is the concern of the discussion on development of end user computing systems.

ENVIRONMENTAL ISSUES

1. Is the end user computing development environment fully described? Have data base, operating systems, hardware, and so on been defined?

    Issue: If the basic operational and development environment has not been defined, the developer must first establish the basics. Because many processing and development options are greatly influenced by what can be processed and the way processing is done, these stage-setting issues must be decided at the outset.

    Generally, the first cut at deciding how to build a system centers around understanding the environment in which the system will be built and run.

2. Once the basic operating and development environments have been determined, what capacity will be available? Who are the other users of the same resources? Will processing resources be available as needed?

    Issue: Even though capacity requirements may not have been estimated as of this moment, it is a good idea to find out which other users will be sharing the same resources. If it appears there may be a conflict, it is appropriate to more closely define the capacity requirements and match them against available resources. Should processing power need to be acquired, there is generally a substantial lead time (for large-scale processors, at least).

3. Have the gross end user computing processing requirements been outlined? Is there a definition of what the final output will address? Has an individual or an end user department been singled out as the judge of the final product?

Issue: The very nature of end user computing is one of ambiguous requirements. Given the ease of iterating end user analysis, it is not necessary to have a rigid set of end user requirements upon embarking on the development of an end user computing system. Indeed, a heuristic development approach for end user computing is often the most productive technique for producing an end product.

Despite the lack of a need for rigid requirements, it is still beneficial to at least roughly outline the general requirements. This gross outline helps to:

Focus the development effort. Without a focus it is easy to wander off onto interesting but unproductive tangents.

Serve as a baseline. Without some definition as to what the final product is to look like, end user computing projects tend to go on and on. It is very useful to have a final target set up at the inception of the project.

4.   Is a new "system of record" being created by the end user computing system?

Issue: In most cases a system of record belongs in the operational environment because of problems of data access, data synchronization, resources required to process the data, compatibility with data architecture, and so forth. There are a few limited instances wherein a system of record can legitimately be built in the end user computing environment. Three conditions must be satisfied:

The volume of data is manageable.

The volume of processing is manageable.

The usage of the data does not extend beyond the immediate boundaries of the end user for whom the system is built.

5.   Have the general requirements been identified in the context of the end user computing architecture? If not, should the architecture be expanded? If so, what architectural considerations are there? Conformity to the architecture of the system being built is important. Every end user must go through this analysis for every new system. If the

end user can build on previous systems that fit within the architecture, then the new system should not reinvent the wheel. If end user data already exists that can be used, then it should be used. There is a real need to carefully proliferate data and systems; otherwise the effectiveness of an architected approach is lost.

6. Once the final system is produced, will the system be run periodically, or will the system be run only once?

   Issue: If the end user computing system is to be run more than once, does it make sense to use traditional development methods? If the system is to be run repeatedly, who will do the running—the end user or computer operations? If computer operations is to do the running, is the software/hardware environment appropriate? What documentation is required? What testing is required? What advance notice does operations need? What capacity will be required?

7. Is the end user computing system that is being built going to pass data to or receive data from another end user computing system? If so, have the format, content, and media on which passage will occur been established? What kind of timing considerations are there?

   Issue: If an end user is building a system solely for himself or herself, then there is no issue of external requirements. But if the system is used to feed other systems or to receive data from other systems, then the issues of the specific interfaces between the two systems must be addressed.

Input Specifications

1. What is the source of data for the end user computing system?

   Issue: Before detailed processing plans can be specified, it is necessary to know the specific content and format of the data that serves as input to processing. Until the developer knows what data is available, little specific development planning and design can occur.

2.   Is the source of input consistent with the architecture for end user computing? Is other data that conforms to the architecture that is already in existence going to be used?

     Issue: Conformance to architecture, especially for the source of data, is critical if the goals of data accuracy and consistency are to be realized. When data is extracted and proliferated in an uncontrolled fashion, there is very little chance that the analysis done for end user computing will be consistent across the entire environment. Without consistency across the environment, there is little chance for effectiveness. It is therefore crucial that the input to end user computing be consistent with the architecture.

3.   How much data is to be input? In what order? On tape? On DASD?

     Issue: The volume of data and its format are major issues of end user computing, especially where a microprocessor is used. If there is too much data, either a subset must be selected, or the data needs to be summarized or otherwise refined. But the time to discover problems is before the program goes into execution.

     The medium on which the data resides is a somewhat less burning issue but is still important. The physical inputing of data at the physical level depends on the medium on which the data is stored. The processor needs to be compatible with the input form. This issue, like the issue of data volume, needs to be addressed early on in the system development life cycle.

4.   Are the assumptions, limitations, refinements, and restrictions of the input defined?

     Issue: The results of end user computing are no better than the input used in the analysis. The first step toward effective input is architectural conformance. But at a more detailed level, the algorithmic extract information, the physical source of extract, the timing of the extract, any restrictions on usage, and so forth are likewise relevant to the clear definition of the input.

5. To what extent has documentation been built and maintained?

    Issue: Documentation is always useful. But in the case of end user computing, and especially in the case of an architected end user computing environment, documentation is extremely important. The essence of an architected environment is the building upon (not over!) previous processing efforts. Without adequate documentation it is very difficult to base future efforts on the current foundation. At a minimum the documentation of input should include:

    Where (in the architecture) the data fits.

    The specific source.

    The extract algorithms used.

    The exact format of the data.

    A verbal description of what the input represents.

    A verbal description of what refinement will be done to the data to produce one or more subsets.

6. Are more than one sources of input to be used? If so, what criteria will be used to merge the data? What will be done about records that should be matched but are not? What problems with matching criteria and the timing of the extract are there? Are any "intersection" calculations to be made? If so, how are they to be calculated? Does the merging of the two sources conform to the architecture? If not, why not?

    Issue: If the input to end user computing is a single source, many processing issues are simplified. But when the input is two or more sources, and those sources need to be merged, sorted, or otherwise refined, the processing that must occur can be complex. Indeed, the end user may wish to design a front end that does nothing but process the different sources of input into a single file.

Output

After the input is established, it is useful to establish the output requirements. Output generally comes in two forms—analytical results and stored output, ready to be used for further processing.

1. Specifically, what output is desired? What is the format of the output?

    Issue: The entire development effort is focused when there is a clear vision of what is required in the way of output. But the nature of end user computing is such that often the specific output is only generally envisioned. In this case, it is very useful to pinpoint as many criteria for satisfaction as possible at the outset of end user computing system development. When the output is defined and when the input is defined, the processing required usually becomes obvious, even when the processing is quite complex.

2. What output is to be stored for future usage? At what level of detail?

    Issue: It is useful to store information for future use and comparison. The results can be stored in manual (or paper) form or can be stored in an electronically compatible form, such as on tape or disk. If trends are to be developed, if patterns are to be measured at a later time, the issues of storage must be addressed at the point of end user computing development. For information that is to be used for trend analysis at a later time, it is often useful to store the information in as detailed a format as is economical so that later analyses can reformat and/or redefine the basic data used to achieve the final result. Once the detail is set, it is expensive to recreate the detail so that a flexible analysis can be done.

3. How does the output to be stored for future usage conform to the end user computing architecture? Does the output recreate in part or all of other end user computing output? If so, how are the differences to be reconciled?

    Issue: The stored output of end user computing represents an important aspect of end user computing. But like all other major components of the end user computing environment, there is the question of how the results conform to the architecture. If there is other data in the end user computing environment that is identical or strongly parallel to the output being produced, this question is raised: Why doesn't the system being built use existing analysis and data?

4. Are archival files being created?

    Issues: The issues of archival files center around the level of detail to be stored, the amount of data to be stored, the frequency with which archival data will be added, the sequence in which archival data will be stored, the final purge criteria from the archival file, the media on which archival data is stored, and the conformance to the architecture.

5. What is the cost of reiterating end user computing analysis?

    Issue: The nature of end user computing is to reiterate analysis until the right results are obtained. As the developer is designing the output, a relevant question becomes: What is the cost of a reiteration? If the cost is very cheap, the designer can afford to loosely specify the final output. But if the execution and reiteration of the system is expensive, the end user ought to design the final output as carefully as is possible.

6. What documentation is there/will there be for the final output?

    Issue: As in the case of input, documentation of output is critical. At a minimum the following should be documented:

    The exact format of the stored output.

    The source(s) of input used to create the output.

    The end user computing system used to create the output.

    Who the end user developers are.

    The date of the system development.

    The date of system execution.

A verbal description of what the data represents.

A verbal description of any limitations.

7.   Are intermediate results to be stored?

Issue: Even though intermediate results may not be construed as output, they can play an invaluable role in the development of end user computing systems. The first (and probably most important) role they play is that of preventing end user computing from having to return to square one in the eventuality of an unsuccessful analysis. The storage of intermediate results allows the end user to have a fallback position in the development of a system. But the storage of intermediate results may also represent the embodiment of some part of the end user computing architecture. By storing the intermediate result, some future end user project may use the intermediate result as input, thus saving considerable processing and development effort, as well as preserving the consistency of the data.

Algorithms

Once the environment, input, and output are defined, the processing algorithms are almost (but not really!) trivial.

1.   What overall structure is there for the processing algorithms for the end user computing system? For the individual components of the system?

Issue: For large end user computing systems, it is useful to outline the general processing strategy, which may encompass more than one program. Then for each program (or each module in a large program) it is useful to document the detailed processing. Included should be such things as comparisons, summarizations, subtotals, detailed calculations, and so forth. Equally as important as the calculations are the verbal descriptions underlying the algorithms. The rationale behind the algorithm is extremely useful should there be a later analysis of the end user computing system.

2. How easy is the system to change, once developed?

   Issue: Given the need of the end user to reiterate executions of the system, it makes sense to create systems that are as changeable as possible. The variables most likely to change are identified and are sensitized to change by one of two means:

   Programs are parametrically controlled. The major variables are represented as parametrically controlled values. To change a value then requires only that the value of the parameter be changed, not that the program be rebuilt.

   Tables are used to contain major variables. Each time the variable is used, it is looked up in the table. There is no need to reprogram the system in order to change a variable. Only the contents of the table need be changed to execute another reiteration of the system.

3. What audit trails are there?

   Issue: For some types of end user computing, it is absolutely essential that there be an audit trail. In these cases, the algorithms used, intermediate results, documentation of input and output all serve as audit tools.

4. What user exits are there?

   Issues: For some end user computing systems, there is a need to do processing that cannot normally or easily be accomplished by standard end user computing software. In these cases a "user exit" is involved. A user exit is a custom-written piece of software that is called by the end user computing software. Once the exit goes into execution, it can process data or do calculations as needed. User exits are typically written in assembler language, COBOL, PL-1, Fortran, and so on. User exits need to be carefully identified and documented.

5. What algorithmic accuracy is required?

   Issue: The simplicity of end user computing software often masks detailed underlying issues. One such issue is the underlying storage and manipulation of numbers. For banking and financial calculations, placement of decimals, rounding algorithm, maximum number to be stored, and so on—all require careful attention.

6.   What temporary storage of data is required?

Issue: Temporary fields are often useful. But these fields escape the same emphasis and attention as normal input and output. The algorithms associated with these fields, the content and usage, and the input to these fields are all useful documentation.

Critical Success Factors/ Guidelines for Effective End User Computing

• •

The end user computing environment is a world in transition. From an industry perspective, the world of end user computing is an immature world, although it is rapidly maturing. Because of changes, new technologies, new economies of scale and of work, the parameters of success are constantly being readjusted. The following guidelines are meant to give some broad direction and definition to the world of end user computing.

The path to effective end user computing has many obstacles. The following short list (in random order) is intended to alert the reader to the most salient factors in the long-term establishment and success of the effective end user computing environment.

1. Shift budgetary responsibility directly to the end user. As long as data processing assumes the traditional role of paying for end user computing resources, the end user has no real, direct responsibility for resources consumed. Given the amount of resources that are typically consumed by the end user, there needs to be feedback to the end user in the form of fiscal responsibility. Such direct responsibility is not unreasonable given the autonomous nature of end user computing.

2.   The development of the end user architecture must be an end user/data processing joint effort. When the architected end user environment becomes exclusively either a data processing effort or an end user effort, there is real jeopardy that the new environment will be ineffective. Naturally end user input is needed in management and direction of the environment. The influence of data processing is likewise mandatory, since it is data processing that feeds data to the end user. Furthermore data processing can contribute the wisdom of having dealt with technology for many years. The most successful end user computing environments are those where there is input and contribution from both the end user and data processing.

3.   As in any organizational endeavor, there is a need to staff personnel carefully. The leaders of the end user computing environment need to have, as a minimum, the following traits:

Leadership.

Communication abilities.

A business awareness.

A technical foundation.

Patience.

An awareness of the economics involved.

An end user perspective.

An ability to understand short-term and long-term goals and perspectives.

4.   The quality of the architecture and the understanding that execution of the architecture is as important as the quality of the architecture are absolutely essential to establishing the effective environment. A quality end user computing architecture will:

Clearly outline the major issues.

Clearly prioritize the major issues.

Remove extraneous detail from consideration.

5.   Management education, feedback, and support are essential to the establishment of the effective end user com-

puting environment. The world of end user computing is so new that changes are happening at a frightfully rapid pace. Today's manager coping with the issues of end user computing is assaulted by choices—of hardware, software, new techniques, and so forth. At the same time, the world of end user computing is in upheaval. To try to cope with, or even keep up with, the furious pace of end user computing, management needs all the help it can get. To this end the personnel in charge of establishing and maintaining the end user computing environment need to pay special attention to the issues of management communication and education.

6. The separation of the different modes of operation—operational and end user computing—is essential in the face of much data and/or much processing. The frustration that can result when trying to merge or marry the two environments is simply unnecessary in the face of volumes of data and/or processing. Where there is a limited amount of data and processing, it is entirely possible that the two modes of operation may be harnessed together on the same processor. But in the usual case, it makes sense to physically separate the two environments. It is critical that a shop not waste resources trying to achieve a theoretical goal of a single source of data for all purposes, as long as there remains a single system of record.

7. The orientation of the atomic DSS data bases needs to be along the lines of subject data bases. The subject data base orientation, along with the detailed granularity of atomic DSS data bases, ensures that the departmental data bases that feed off of the atomic DSS data bases have the utmost flexibility. The granularity of the data allows the data to be extracted and sorted in any way the data *can* be sorted. The subject data base orientation ensures the data is organized in an accessible, understandable fashion. It is critical to the flexibility of the departmental and individual end user computer processing that data be organized this way.

8. If not absolutely critical, it is at least a very good idea to move end user computing to the smallest processor that

will suffice at least at the outset of end user computing. It is assumed that the end user can move up in processor size if needed, within the line of processor originally chosen. But it is also assumed that the end user will consume whatever resources are allocated. Consequently, to control resource utilization, it is good practice initially to put the end user on the smallest processor that will suffice.

9. It is critical to control the proliferation of departmental data bases. There is redundancy of data among departmental data bases, but that redundancy does not mean that there should not be a sharing of data at the departmental level. Where there is a commonality of needs at the departmental level, there needs to be sharing of data. Otherwise, departmental "sprawl" will occur, wasting resources and further diluting the accuracy and believability of the data.

10. The building of operational systems with decision support tools should strongly be discouraged. The only possible rationale for building operational systems (or "systems of records") outside of the standard operational arena is when *all* of the following criteria are satisfied:

    The volume of data is limited.

    The volume of processing is limited.

    The data that forms the backbone of the system has no use, application, or interest outside the immediate end users who are developing the system.

11. There is one clearly defined system of record. The system of record is the final authority, on a detailed data basis, as to the accuracy and up-to-the-second content of data. Unless there are very unusual circumstances, the system of record environment should be entirely contained in the operational environment. Many resources and types of resources are wasted in the attempt to maintain multiple systems of record.

12. The most cost-effective usage of end user computing is to funnel the most resources in the most critical parts of the business. The effectiveness of end user computing is questionable when end user computing is being used for activities tangential to the crucial aspects of the business.

In other words, the biggest payback to end user computing occurs when it is aimed at the most important, most sensitive aspects of the business.

13. The worth of end user computing can be measured in terms of effectiveness and in terms of efficiency. Effectiveness is best measured by the general prosperity indicators of a company. Only in isolated cases can effectiveness be measured directly. Efficiency can be measured by comparing the differential in the development and operational costs of traditional tools compared to end user computing tools.

14. It is easy to mistake the solutions of effective end user computing with the tools used to achieve those solutions. No software, no methodology, no architecture is a replacement for human understanding and management of the issues.